AGAINST ALL ODDS

The Story of How a Group of Young Men Captured the Heart of a Campus

DAVE SCRIBNER

With Technical Assistance by

PAUL J. MROZ Ph.D.

ISBN 979-8-89345-658-5 (paperback)
ISBN 979-8-89345-659-2 (digital)

Christian Faith Publishing
832 Park Avenue
Meadville, PA 16335
www.christianfaithpublishing.com

Printed in the United States of America

CONTENTS

SECTION 1

SECTION 2

FOREWORD

AGAINST ALL ODDS

**The Story of How a Group of Young Men
Captured the Heart of a Campus
A book by author Dave Scribner
About The 1965-67 Roberts Wesleyan College
Athletic Hall of Fame Basketball Team**

This book chronicles the story of a championship basketball team, and how an inspired group of young college athletes achieved their dreams of success. It reveals the early history of each member of the team, from their formative years through their college experiences. It culminates with players' personal reflections over 50 years with the team's induction into the Roberts Wesleyan University Athletic Hall of Fame in 2017.

It reveals a primitive conditioning environment lacking not only a gym, but also a weight and training room, along with little financial program support in the mid 1960's. Coaches and players learned to endure and overcome these conditions developing an overcoming attitude and spirit that would serve them well in high pressure game situations.

The story culminates with many 50-year reflections which summarizes life lessons related to and associated with their college experiences. This athletic story chronicles important universal practices and beliefs for living a successful meaningful life.

Athletes, if you strive for excellence, desire to excel athletically, have future college aspirations, and are planning to play college sports, this book is for you.

Coaches, if you desire to inspire young athletes with examples of athletic success and are interested in character building, this book is for you.

Community leaders, if you are interested in highlighting positive community role models and the athletic accomplishments of former local athletes who have benefitted from your recreation programs, this book is for you.

Alumni, students and university athletes, these individual reflections reveal not only the history of Roberts Wesleyan athletics in the mid-1960's but also highlight the character of Roberts graduates and the nature and endurance of the college spirit. Today, Roberts' is recognized as the leading institution for character education in New York State. Character mattered then, and character matters today. If character matters to you, this book is for you.

Paul J. Mroz. Ph.D.
1966-67 Team Manager

SETTING

The main setting for this saga is the campus of Roberts Wesleyan University, located in North Chili, New York, approximately ten miles west of Rochester. The school was founded in 1866 by the Reverend B. T. Roberts. The institution evolved from a seminary to a junior college (1945) to a senior college (1949). Between the years 1949 and 2023, the school was known as Roberts Wesleyan College. Roberts is a Liberal Arts college in the Christian tradition.

This story takes place during the years of 1965 through 1967. The '60s were an exciting time for the college. Under the leadership of President Dr. Elwood Voller, the college experienced a period of unprecedented growth. During his eleven years at the helm (1957–1968), Dr. Voller more than doubled the college's physical plant by adding fifteen buildings and doubling the enrollment from 360 to 750.

Also, during those halcyon days, intercollegiate athletics began to play a vital role in the life of the college. Men's teams were fielded in cross-country, soccer, basketball, and track and field. Considering the small size of our student body and our lack of athletic facilities (we did not even have a field house), it is amazing how well some of these teams performed. The cross-country team won five consecutive state titles and thirty-three consecutive duel and triangular meets. The soccer team made it to the NAIA national tournament in 1966. You will read how well the basketball team performed in the next few pages. It was also a time of unparalleled excellence in other parts of the college, such as music and nursing. The Roberts Chorale was invited to tour Europe. The nursing program was recognized as a top program in New York State.

This was the environment from which the 1965–1967 men's basketball emerged and flourished. As Stan Ziblut, our starting point guard, said, "It was a great time to be a Raider."

PREFACE

Periodically, a college produces an athletic team that surpasses all expectations and all statistical standards recorded to date. The entire college community becomes mesmerized by the team and attendance soars.

Such a phenomenon occurred at Roberts Wesleyan College (now known as Roberts Wesleyan University) between 1965 and 1967 when the men's basketball team won thirty-eight of forty-four games, set many school records (including sixteen wins in a row), received a post-season tournament bid each year, and played every home game in front of a sellout crowd.

Many contend that this kind of phenomenon does not just happen. There are reasons, and there are factors. This book will attempt to identify the reasons and factors that led to the success of this team. This book will tell a story about the genesis of this team and how the individuals on the team developed, came together, and learned how to play team basketball under the guidance of a firm and dedicated coach. Conclusions may be drawn because this is not a scientific study. Any conclusions drawn will have limitations.

WHY THIS BOOK?

Here are the two reasons:

1. There is a story here that needs to be told. Yes, these young men came together from a myriad of backgrounds and places, such as Chaffee, New York, and demonstrated the true meaning of sacrifice and teamwork. Yes, these young men won 86 percent of their games. They held fourteen of seventeen team records. But how did that come to be? How were they able to sacrifice their own goals and embrace the greater goals of the team? Why are they so close today? The answers beg to be found, and it has been a privilege for me to search for and find many of them.

2. The college should have this story recorded for future generations to contemplate and enjoy. Just as Neil Pfouts wrote an excellent treatise entitled *A History of Roberts Wesleyan College*, this book will serve to document the excellence that this team achieved at that point in time and how they achieved it. A copy of this book hopefully will be ensconced in the Golisano Library pending certain approvals. Hopefully, this will provide a roadmap for other coaches and players who sincerely wish to experience the success that we experienced on and off the court. The values that we model are timeless, and we believe they are transferable.

WHO WILL TELL THE STORY?

The story will be told from a unique vantage point. Dave Scribner (the author), who never played high school ball, not only won a roster spot on the team but also earned a spot in the rotation and contributed significantly to the team's success. Dave will provide the reader with a background on each player and the coach. He will explore the special qualities his teammates possessed, which enabled them to help this team win. He will explain what it was like to play for Coach Hughes and how the Coach inspired him to give his absolute best each minute he was on the court. You will see this team through the eyes of Dave.

Dave will also take you into the actual games and give the reader a flavor of what it was like to be on the court against some great rivals like Buffalo State. He will tell what he felt in his heart when the team was welcomed home by hundreds of fans lining the streets of North Chili following a devastating loss to Millersville State in the NAIA District thirty-two finals.

He will also tackle the following questions:

- Why did these players come to Roberts, and from where did they come?
- What qualities enabled them to make and play on this team?
- What special role did each player fulfill?
- How did this experience affect their lives?
- How do they feel about their experience on the team as they look back on the experience fifty years later?

Collection of Data

Data was collected on the historical roots and the personal journeys of the various members of the Roberts Wesleyan College, 1965–'67, Hall of Fame Basketball Team. Over one hundred personal interviews were conducted with players and anyone who knew them as young athletes. Other sources of data included newspaper articles, scorecard inserts, college yearbooks, and Athletic Department records. This team was recently named the greatest team in the history of the college and the first team to be inducted into the college's Athletic Hall of Fame in its entirety. The book will examine the commonalities as well as the differences that these young men brought to the team. The book will document what made this team great and why the team left such a great impact on the students, faculty, administration, and the community.

The author owes a special debt to Harry Hutt, who was the Sports Information Director during this team's reign of excellence. Harry created all the program inserts, press releases, and press guides. These documents were full and overflowing with robust statistics and insights. I referred to this information on many occasions as I wrote the book. I am not surprised that Harry went on to a great career in public relations and marketing with several teams in the NBA and the NHL.

Sadly, we lost Harry in 2022. More information on Harry is provided later in the book.

Introduction by the Author (Dave)

This book is a story about a great basketball team and the coach who brought the team together. I had the privilege of being on this team, so of course, I was able to see everything that happened from the time practice started in early October until the last game was played in early March. Every practice and every game served as a laboratory for me to learn more and more about this sport that I had fallen in love with—BASKETBALL.

I also came to love a great group of guys who were developing a commitment to each other and a commitment to playing winning basketball. The more these guys listened to the inspiring messages of the coach, the harder they worked and the more they won. In 1964–65, this group of guys delivered the first winning season to Roberts in four years when they went 13–6. Going into the '65–'66 season and retaining several starters, they were on the verge of greatness, and the team sensed it. I was bound and determined to earn a spot on this team. I practiced the fundamentals of basketball during most of my free time. I worked on my crossover dribble until I was totally confident that I could use it against any opponent. No opponent was going to steal the ball from me. If he went for a steal, I would speed by him, and he would have to pay.

That fall of '65, I was also falling in love with a small liberal arts college on the outskirts of Rochester, New York. I was intrigued by the interesting people who attended Roberts Wesleyan College. Many of them became life-long friends. I would spend the next four years there. I learned that most of those people were avid basketball fans, and in a couple of months, they would pack the gym at the Churchville-Chili High School, cheering the Raiders (as we were known then) on to another victory. It was a tremendous privilege for me to play in front of these fans.

Another part of the story is about what I saw and what I experienced each and every day as a key player on this team. I saw all the little things that the coach had us do that resulted in playing winning basketball. As I sit here and type these words and thoughts, warm memories float in my brain. I cannot wait to tell this story. I could never have made up a story as improbable as this story. Sometimes, I pinch myself just to reaffirm that it happened. I thank God that it did.

It is also a story about the wonderful people who swept me along on this fairy-tale, story-book journey to the pinnacle of small college basketball. I will be forever indebted to those people. I went from being an athletic nobody as an incoming freshman at Roberts Wesleyan College to being inducted into the college's Athletic Hall of Fame with my team in its entirety fifty years later. I would like to thank everybody who was a part of my journey and for the role they played in my career, including my Coach, Bill Hughes, a man I will always admire and respect until the day I die. I thank God for bringing Coach Hughes to Roberts Wesleyan College.

In this story, I will also tell you about each of my teammates, the greatest teammates a player could ask for. I will tell you about the memorable games in which I participated, including a game against Buffalo State when five hundred people were turned away at the door because the fire marshals had to follow the safety codes. I will tell you about the night that one of my teammates scored 54 points and was named King of Winter Weekend the same day. But most of all, I want to tell you about all the things I observed daily, especially the coaching style of Bill Hughes and the values he instilled in the team. I saw a no-nonsense, business-like approach to the game of basketball. The coach's values were about discipline, setting goals, and character. The coach modeled these values at all team functions and activities. The coach never let us forget that we were representing Roberts Wesleyan College, a Christian College, and that it was a privilege to do so. The players bought into these values and with Coach Hughes leading the way, the team rose to some dizzying heights.

I saw it all. I listened to it all. What a thrill it was for me to be on this team. I savored every minute. This team was so special that there was probably not a young man on campus who wouldn't have loved to have been on it. I was a very lucky young man to have been there at the time I was. The timing was perfect. Had I been a few years earlier or a few years later, I would have missed it all. But I was there, and I was there at the right time. I was in the thick of battle in every game. The team needed a point guard to come off the bench, handle the ball, play pressure man-to-man defense, start our famous Carson-Newman shuffle offense, and get the ball to the open man. Those were the exact skills I had.

I hope you enjoy going on this journey with me and my team. If you were a fan, believe me, we loved you, and we loved your passion. This passion and the thunderous vocal support you generated were probably worth twenty points a game. There was one especially great fan by the name of Leon Caster, and every time I entered a game, he would yell out, "Let's go, Scribby." I was too cool to let him know that I heard him, but I did hear him. His words gave me tremendous motivation. The fans would follow us to road games, and sometimes, we would have more fans in an away arena than the home team.

If you have never heard of Roberts Wesleyan College, come along with me, and I will tell you why this school was the perfect incubating ground for developing a championship team. I will tell you about the faculty, the administration, and the alumni, and how they showered love on our team. I will tell you how we accomplished this without even having our own gym.

As I think of my story, I often burst into tears because what happened to me was so wonderful and great. I met the most beautiful woman in the world at Roberts, and Mary Kay became my wife and best friend. We have been married for forty-eight years. What more could I ask for? But before I tell the story, I must tell you how my basketball career was distinctly different from the careers of my teammates. I must tell you something about the huge void that was in my basketball resume—something that gave me great pain. Here is the answer.

I never played high school ball!

Not one minute. How could a guy like me who did not play ball in high school not only make a college team but make a great team as well and then earn a spot in the rotation? Many players who play in high school come to college hoping to play. Often, they are outsized, outmuscled, or lacking in quickness. They are good but not good enough. I was fortunate to be a natural point guard. At five feet ten inches, I could play the position and hold my own. I was scrappy. I was good enough, and I proved it with the grace of God. But please don't think I did not pick up a basketball until I got to college. I played for years at the Batavia, New York, YMCA, not the school. I will tell you why later. The Batavia YMCA was where I learned the game and honed my skills. I was not extremely talented, but I worked incredibly hard.

CHAPTER 1

If You Build It, They Will Come

The heading above comes from the baseball movie *Field of Dreams*. I would like to borrow it because it was true for our team. With Coach Hughes being the architect, we built a winning, dominant team, and the fans came from all over.

This was a great team. There is no question that this group of young men under the leadership of Coach Hughes made a tremendous impact on the college. But let's look at one parameter of greatness, which is universal in sports. How many people come to watch the team play (bodies in the seats)? Few people, other than friends and family, come to see a losing team. A five hundred team will draw some fans, but not a lot. A truly great team will pack the place out.

Let's look at the '65–'67 teams. Unless one counts games played during the '40s and '50s in the Carpenter Hall "pit," there has never been an era in Robert's basketball history when sellouts were the rule. During the two special years of '65–'67, the stands were full for all home games. It was standing room only. Not only that, when we were on the road, it was true that there often were as many Roberts fans who showed up as there were fans for the home team.

From 1965–67, the Roberts team played in front of full houses in every home game. Home games were played at Churchville-Chili High School, which seated approximately one thousand people. There were twenty home games in that stretch, which means that approximately twenty thousand attendees saw these Raiders.

Game attendees included the following:

- *Students*. Probably made up 60–65 percent of the game attendees. Many students would arrive thirty minutes before the scheduled tip-off. Reason? They wanted to watch us warm up. Our warm-ups were really entertaining, especially the dunking drill. There were seven guys on the team who could dunk, which in the sixties was a big deal.
- *Faculty*. The faculty were regular attendees at the games. Often during the week, a faculty member would stop me on campus and ask about the team and how we were doing. I loved it when that happened. It told me that the faculty members knew who I was and cared about the team. French Professor Elsa Logan would sit in the second row and cheer enthusiastically and vociferously in an uninhibited way. The team loved it, and they loved her. By the way, I hope she would approve of my writing in this book. She taught me how to write.
- *Administration*. The college President, Dr. Elwood Voller, came to all home games and some away games as well. His cabinet also attended.
- *Alumni*. Robert's grads who lived in the area were enthusiastic fans.
- *Members of Pearce Church* (the college-associated church)
- *Community*
- *Parents and family*

During the subsequent fifty-five years, Roberts played primarily at two venues:

- Churchville-Chili Gymnasium (old and new)
- Voller Athletic Center

I think it is safe to say that the Roberts Wesleyan Men's Basketball teams have never had even one sellout at the Voller Athletic Center. This is not meant in any way to be a criticism of these teams. It merely shows how special the '65–'67 team was.

Meet the Players

Scope

This book covers two seasons, 1965–66 and 1966–67. The players who graduated after playing on the '65–'66 team included:

- Herman Schwingle
- Stan Ziblut
- Bob Ahlin

The players who played on both teams ('65-'67) included:

- Keith Moore
- Frank Carter
- Bill Bachmann
- Dale Easterly
- Glen Schultz
- Noel Smith
- Ken Curtis
- Dave Scribner (Dave spent most of the first year on the Freshman team).

The players who played on the '66–'67 team included:

- Paul Crowell
- Ralph Roach
- Darwin Chapman

The 1966–1967 championship team.
Back row: Paul Mroz (manager), Ken Curtis, Paul Crowell, Bill
Bachmann, Noel Smith, Glenn Schultz, Head Coach Bill Hughes
Kneeling row: Dale Easterly, Keith Moore, Frank
Carter, Ken Page, Dave Scribner

CHAPTER 2

A Prolific Scorer from the Grape Country
Herman Schwingle

Nestled in the Italy Hills, approximately forty miles south of Rochester, New York, lies the quaint and picturesque village of Naples. Naples is well-known for its annual trout derby in the spring and its grape festival in the fall. It is right on the edge of the thriving Finger Lakes wine industry. No one would ever expect that Naples and the surrounding area could have been a breeding ground for outstanding college basketball players. Meet Herman Schwingle. He grew up in Naples and starred for his Naples High School team in the early '60s, as he led his team to win after win and drew in enough surrounding townspeople to assure sellout crowds for every home game. He once scored 16 points in the first quarter of a game. As a sophomore on his Naples team, he was sixth man. That team won the Class C Sectionals while going undefeated. A very small school, Naples, had only forty students in each class.

I spoke to several local citizens about the kind of player Herman was and what kind of crucible shaped his development and enabled him to become a Hall-of-Fame player for Roberts Wesleyan College, where he enrolled as a freshman in 1962. First and foremost, Herman played ball anytime he could get in a gym. If he and his friends could not get in a gym, they would go to one of several nearby barns that had a basket.

Townspeople extolled his commitment to excellence and his work ethic. Herman was a physical fitness fanatic. Now I never saw him do this, but I am told that Herman could stand on his hands and then do pushups from that upside-down position. Herman probably was the most physically fit player on the team. He would put on ankle weights and a weight vest and run the hills around Naples. Paul Curtis, a lifelong friend of mine and a Roberts' graduate, remembers Herman walking to classes wearing ankle weights. At one point during the offseason, Herman took a job at Taylor Instrument in Rochester. Taylor Instrument was about ten miles from campus. Herman would jog to and from work.

Herman starred as a soccer goalie before handing the job over to Dale Easterly. He was inducted into the Roberts Athletic Hall of Fame twice, once for his own individual achievements and once as a member of the greatest team in the school's history.

Herman grew up in a family that attended church regularly. He was also involved in Youth for Christ. He marched to his own drummer. According to Coach Hughes, he was unique because of his uniqueness. Everyone loved Herman, and everyone always will.

Role on the Team

Herman was one of the best outside shooters on the team. His job was to score points, and during his junior year, he did just that. If the three-point shot had been instituted back then, Herman might have averaged twenty-five points per game. I do not mean to imply that Herman was a gunner. He was not. He just was not afraid to take any shot. He also had a remarkable ability to meld with the team, whether on a fast break or engaging in the shuffle offense. He was smooth and polished.

Swingle drives for a layup.

CHAPTER 3

State Champ Keith Moore

The 1969 World Series featured the New York Mets and the Baltimore Orioles. The Orioles were not only the best team in the American League; they were perhaps the greatest Oriole team of all time. The Mets were baseball's "lovable losers" during the '60s. Founded in 1962 as an expansion team, they were considered lucky to be there. This was the Mets's first winning season ever.

The Orioles won game one, but the Mets surprisingly won games two and three. In the fourth game, the Mets had the lead, but the Orioles were rallying. With runners in scoring position, future Hall of Famer Brooks Robinson hit a sinking line drive to right field that looked like a sure extra-base hit that would have put the O's ahead. However, a Mets player by the name of Ron Swoboda came out of nowhere and made one of the greatest catches in World Series history by diving on the ground and snagging the ball inches above the turf. The catch prevented the Orioles from taking the lead and the Mets went on to win game four. Ron Swoboda continued his heroics in game five. In the eighth inning, he doubled in Cleon Jones with the go-ahead run. An inning later, the game was over, and the Mets were world champs. It was one of the greatest upsets in the history of sports, and Ron Swoboda became a World Series hero and a household name.

Now you are probably wondering why I am including this story in a book about the '65–'67 Roberts Wesleyan basketball team. The answer can be found in the following trivia question:

What do Ron Swoboda and Dave Scribner (this book's Author) have in common?

Answer: They both played basketball in the same backcourt with Keith Moore.

Dave played with Keith at Roberts Wesleyan College, and Ron and Keith started in the backcourt at Sparrows Point High School in Sparrows Point, Maryland.

Keith Moore was one of the best guards ever to wear the Roberts uniform. Blessed with natural speed and quickness (both of which were deceptive), he was named to the Roberts Athletic Hall of Fame in 2013. During his senior year, I had the privilege of playing with Keith. Usually, I would come off the bench to give Keith a rest, but often, I subbed for another player, and Keith and I were together in the backcourt. He was a pleasure to play with. I also had the unenviable task of guarding him in practice. He would score at will on me. In order to look good to Coach Hughes, I would have to grab his shirt and hold him on occasion. He didn't like it. I don't blame him. I didn't like him scoring on me, but I was desperate.

During his last two years, he averaged eleven points per game. However, everyone knew that his points per game average would have been much higher had Frank Carter and Bill Bachmann, two of the greatest players in Roberts' history, not been on the team. But Keith was a team player all the way. He knew when to assert himself, and he also knew when to pull back. Players picked Keith to be cocaptain his senior year. The respect he earned over the previous two years had a lot to do with it.

Certain adjectives pop into my mind as I think of Keith. He was slick. He was steady. He had a good basketball IQ. Poise, polished, and competitive also come to mind. But as I watched him play, I sensed a special quality that went beyond the skills and fundamentals of the game. His movements on the court had an aesthetic quality that is not often seen. He drove to the basket with flair and enthusiasm.

Now let's switch gears for a moment and get back to *Ron Swoboda*. Swoboda must have known something about winning because seven years before, he became a World Series legend. He played on the State Championship team at Sparrows Point High School in Sparrows Point, Maryland. Keith Moore was a key player on that team. Swoboda was a junior. Keith Moore was a senior.

I spoke with *Swoboda* on the phone in preparation for writing this book. After getting over some nervousness about speaking with a World Series legend, I settled down and asked what it was like to play with Keith. Ron was very complementary in everything he said. He mentioned that he looked up to Keith and that Keith often mentored him. He also said that Keith had a very high basketball IQ. It was obvious to me that these two high achievers have remained friends over the years.

Many of the players came to Roberts with good high school basketball credentials. However, no one could claim to have been a starter on a state championship team—Keith Moore could.

Role on the Team

There is no question about the leadership skills that Keith Moore brought to the team. However, we also had other strong leaders on the team, such as Frank Carter and Stan Ziblut. I contend that, on this team, Keith Moore served as a perfect shooting guard or two-guard. Here is my argument: Keith was the third leading scorer on the team during his junior and senior years. As a shooter, Keith was also very effective against tough competition. He poured in twenty-one points against Buffalo State.

A Side Path Taken

There is a chapter in the Keith Moore story that is so poignant that I would be remiss not to include it. The positive outcomes from this story reached out over two seasons and probably longer than that when one considers the number of people who knew what happened. I do not mean to be surreptitious about this, so I will tell you what happened as I have been told.

Some players and coaches set their goals and make a beeline to those goals with little fanfare or acrimony. This was not the case with Keith Moore and Bill Hughes. Both player and coach came riding into town in 1961 with guns blazing. Moore, the player, arrived at Roberts after being a key player for Sparrows Point High School as the Maryland School won its only state championship in history. In 1961, Hughes was recently hired by President Elwood Voller to serve as athletic director, director of physical education, classroom instructor, head soccer coach, and head basketball coach. It was a Herculean task, but Bill Hughes had never steered away from challenges. He was not about to do that now.

Moore was brimming with confidence by the accounts I heard, perhaps even bordering on cockiness. It was reported that Keith acted as though he was more of an expert on basketball than the coach. Sometimes, that can be true. But being right is not the issue. The issue is oneness and team unity, characteristics that are vital to winning. No one challenged Coach Hughes without being called out. To make a long story short, the situation became unsustainable, and Hughes called Moore into his office and told him he was no longer on the team, and he told him why. The rest of the conversation was not pretty, and Moore bolted out the door.

This is highly significant because Keith Moore was an outstanding player, and the team needed his skills to achieve a winning season. Coach Hughes certainly realized this, but this was a situation where the coach put principle over expedience. It also sent a strong message to the rest of the team that the coach was willing to act on principle and would not tolerate anyone who did not adhere to his values.

About a year later, Moore was experiencing quite a bit of anguish because of his separation from the team and the game he loved. He asked to meet with the coach in the coach's office. He told the coach that he missed playing on the team and asked to be reinstated. Coach Hughes rarely reinstated a player who was removed from the team for insubordination to the coach. But he sensed a sincerity and a desire from Keith that ran deeply. He told Keith that he would be reinstated for a probationary period and that to remain on the team, Keith would have to do the following:

- Listen to Coach Hughes and do whatever he asks.
- Keep his GPA high.
- Be a positive influence on his teammates.

This saga worked out well for everybody. The team learned that the coach was serious about his approach to basketball. Moore got an opportunity to become one of the greatest guards in the history of the school, and the fans saw win after win. Keith Moore's contributions were huge.

Moore and Carter accept the Grace College Tournament trophy.

CHAPTER 4

The Batavians Noel Smith and Dave Scribner

Background

During the summer of 1961, a Babe Ruth League baseball game was being played between the Alberty Drug Cubs and the Graham Manufacturing Pirates in Batavia, New York. The game was being played on the diamond at MacArthur Stadium, which was also the home of the Class D Batavia Pirates, a minor league affiliate of the Pittsburgh Pirates. Many players who went on to fame in the Major Leagues actually got their start here in Batavia, including future Pirate stars Steve Blass and Manny Sanguillen. Across town at Williams Park, a permanent small stadium existed for the Babe Ruth League, but due to poor field conditions or overscheduling, games were occasionally switched to the more prestigious MacArthur Stadium.

The Game

Pitching often dominated this league, which was designed for twelve- to fifteen-year-old boys, and tonight was no exception. Going into the seventh and last inning, the Cubs had managed only one hit. However, they scratched and clawed enough to manufacture one run, and the score was tied at one apiece as Dave Scribner led off the top of the seventh (the last inning for Babe Ruth League baseball). Facing a fire balling pitcher named Sam Pilato, Scribner lined a pitch over the head of the second baseman for a solid single. The next batter was a tall and rangy fellow by the name of Noel Smith. When he made contact, Noel could hit the ball "a country mile," as Dizzy Dean used to say. But like most power hitters, he was prone to striking out often. His Dad, Stanley N. Smith, was Batavia's Chief of Police. Chief Smith was a great lover of baseball, and he was one of the finest high school and college umpires in the area. The elder Smith also donated his time to umpire in Batavia's youth leagues. Occasionally, Chief Smith was the umpire behind the plate when his son would come to bat. Noel has emphatically stated that he received no favorable calls from his dad and that he often got "rung up" by his dad.

It is not certain if Chief Smith was umpiring that night, nor did it matter. With Scribner taking a big lead off first, Smith hit a screamer down the right-field line. The ball squirted past the right fielder, and Smith chugged around the bases and ended with a triple while driving in Scribner with the lead run while putting the Cubs up, 2–1. Smith subsequently scored on a wild pitch, and the Cubs won, 3–1.

This is a true story. At that point in time, Scribner and Smith were friends. They played on the same baseball team and saw each other perhaps twice a week in the summer. *But neither Scribner nor Smith had any idea what lay before them four years down the road.* No one knew that in another time and place, and while playing another sport, they would have the opportunity to play side-by-side on *the greatest college basketball team ever produced in the seventy-five-year history of the sport at Roberts Wesleyan College.*

Bye-Bye Baseball

The question arises as to what happened to their baseball careers. The answer is nothing. They just sort of dropped out. There was an American Legion League for the sixteen- to eighteen-year-old age group. But neither Smith nor Scribner had much interest. They had each found a new love, and it was basketball. The Batavia YMCA had adequate courts, and there were always guys hanging around the gyms, so it was easy to pick up a game. Both spent hours at the "Y," polishing their basketball skills.

They strode onto the court together for the first time during the '65–'66 season when Roberts took on the University of Toronto in Toronto. Scribner was brought up from the freshman team to get a little seasoning with the varsity. Scribner's first college assist came later in that game when he called for a play that would bring Smith around a double screen while trying to shed his defender. The play worked out perfectly as Smith left his defender stuck in the screen. Upon receiving a pass from Scribner, Smith promptly sank a fifteen-foot jumper. This was the first of many baskets that this pair of "ballers" would hook up for in the years ahead. They were the only players on this team to have played together as teammates in another time and place.

Fifty years later, in September 2017, both Scribner and Smith were inducted[1] into the college's Athletic Hall of Fame as members of the 1965–'67 teams, the first teams ever to be inducted into the Hall of Fame in their entirety. During those two years, the "Raiders" dominated the local college athletic scene as they ran up a record of thirty-eight wins against only six losses.

These two Batavians have remained the best of friends for life. Smith's wife, Winnie, is best friends with Scribner's wife, Mary Kay. Even though they live over a thousand miles apart, they get together as couples at least once a year. They speak on the phone almost every week. It is a fact of life at Roberts that these lifelong friendships are common.

But How Did They Wind Up at Roberts Wesleyan?

Scribner and Smith took circuitous routes to arrive at Roberts. After playing high school basketball, Smith, who had grown to 6–5 with a rugged frame, was recruited to Alfred State University, a two-year school. During his senior year at Batavia High School, Smith was also contacted by Coach Bill Hughes to play ball at Roberts.

---

[1] See article "Two."

He chose Alfred. His lack of experience and limited playing time at Alfred State proved, after one year, that Smith needed a different environment to flourish as a college player. He contacted Coach Hughes and the two set up a meeting. Coach Hughes welcomed him to come to Roberts but promised him nothing in terms of playing time. Noel would have to earn it.

So the pressure was on Noel. He had to redshirt his freshman year because of transfer rules, which meant he could participate in every practice and suit up for every game, but he could not play. It was a tough year, but he persevered, and the experience of practicing with this team under the watchful eye of Coach Hughes made him ready for college ball. Yes, Noel "earned it." Noel played a key role on both the great teams of '65–'66 and '66–'67, often backing up Bill Bachmann. He averaged 3.3 points and 5.0 rebounds per game during his first season of action and 4.1 points and 6.2 rebounds per game the next year. He had a nice touch on his outside shots and was fierce and rugged on the boards. He never backed down to anyone. Scribner took an entirely different route to secure a spot on this team. He never played high school ball. Why not? He was certainly skilled enough. It is a compelling story, and he will tell it shortly.

Bad News

"I'm sorry, son, you have a heart murmur. You can't play basketball." The words of the Batavia school physician pierced through me like a sword cutting through butter. I was stunned. I was crushed. The silent voice within me wanted to yell out, "Hey, wait a minute. Don't you know I already made the jayvee team? I'm destined to start. Playing basketball is what I do best. It is who I am." But instead, I bit my tongue, said nothing, and kept my anger and rage to myself.

The Lord works in mysterious ways. Little did I know what lay before me four years down the road—the opportunity to play basketball on the greatest team, with the greatest teammates, in front of the greatest fans, for the greatest coach in the more than seventy years of intercollegiate basketball at Roberts Wesleyan College. What a twist of fate. My journey was punctuated and then cap-stoned in

September 2017 with induction into the Roberts Wesleyan Athletic Hall of Fame as a member of the first team, in its entirety, to be inducted.

The Four-Year Incubation

As I gradually outgrew the heart murmur, I continued to play basketball throughout my high school years. However, my games were at the Batavia YMCA (not the school), and it was at the "Y" that I honed my basketball skills. I played in the men's industrial league, in the church league for the Methodist team, and on the "Y" travel team. I was a gym rat in the most literal sense of the word. I came to Roberts in the Fall of '65. I first learned about Roberts through several Roberts-educated Assistant Pastors at our church, the Batavia First United Methodist Church. One of these pastors was Don Coburn, class of '59. He was a sharp guy, and to a teenager like me, he seemed to be a wonderful example of Christianity in action. He made Roberts seem attractive to me. I also knew some Batavians who were attending Roberts, including lifelong friend and fellow teammate, Noel Smith, class of '68 (yes, the guy I just described and with whom I played Babe Ruth baseball). I was further attracted to Roberts because of its lifestyle disciplines. I wanted to get an education without being subjected to the pressures of drinking and drugs, which seemed to be prevalent at many other colleges.

Roles on the Team

There is no question about Noel's role on the team. With a body that stretched up to 6–5, broad shoulders, and an attitude that said, "Don't mess with me," he owned the boards. He often subbed for the greatest rebounder in the college's history, Bill Bachmann, and when this happened, the Raiders experienced no drop-off in rebounding performance. They still dominated the boards. So Noel's role was to rebound. I may have been the best ball handler on the team. The coach utilized me as the first guard off the bench, and he expected me to be flawless when it came to bringing the ball up the court, initiat-

17

ing the Carson-Newman shuffle offense, and playing intense defense in our jump-switching pressure man-to-man defense. My role was not to score or rebound. I had a pretty accurate outside shot, so I was not afraid to shoot and keep the defense honest. I made my share.

CHAPTER 5

A Leader from Niagara Falls
Stan Ziblut

Trivia Question: What did Stan Ziblut and Michael Jordan have in common?

Answer: Neither one made his high school team until his junior year.

When you saw the title of this chapter, I am sure that you assumed the chapter was going to be about Frank Carter. True, Frank was from Niagara Falls, and he was a tremendous leader on the team. But this chapter is about Stan Ziblut. Stan left a great legacy after four years at Roberts Wesleyan College. It was not just in athletics that Stan shone. He was very involved with campus life, serving as class president for two years.

I was a freshman when Stan was a senior. Because he was a point guard, he served as a model for me. I wanted to be in the position he was in when I was an upper classman, so I watched him closely. I was impressed by his intensity and his smartness. He always seemed to be in the right place at the right time on the court. He could get the ball to the big guys, and he could consistently hit the medium-range jumper to keep the defense honest.

It is said that Michael Jordan (who was probably the greatest player on the planet during the '80s and the '90s) never made his high school basketball team until his junior year. Before that, he was always cut. From 1962 to 1966, there was an outstanding player at Roberts Wesleyan who experienced the same fate in high school as Michael Jordan. He was cut every year until his junior year. His name was Stan Ziblut. What was the excuse given to Stan on why he was cut every year until his junior year? Stan only stood about five feet tall. He was told by the coaches that he was too short. The fact that his other skills were outstanding did not seem to matter. He was just too short.

Stan, however, was not one to sit around and mope. He kept playing in pickup games or any other place where the players were competitive. In time, his skills could not be overlooked, and he made the team in his junior year. He really blossomed in his senior year at LaSalle, leading the team to a winning season and averaging double figures.

In college, Stan was the starting point guard on the '65–'66 team that went 18–3. That year Stan ran the offense and played an aggressive and stifling defense, especially in the team's half-court zone press. He was steady and poised.

But before he decided to enroll at Roberts, he had to discover Roberts and hear and learn about Roberts. Why would a guy from Niagara Falls who went to a small Catholic high school want to attend a Free Methodist college in Rochester? I asked Stan this question during an interview on January 20, 2023, and he mentioned the name Bill Coleman. Bill Coleman was a starter on the '61–'62 team at Roberts the same year that Coach Hughes arrived. Stan learned about Roberts Wesleyan through Coleman, who also happened to be an outstanding player at La Salle High School a few years earlier. The answer was opportunity. Stan saw many opportunities at Roberts.

He came to Roberts with little fanfare and certainly no athletic scholarship. Yet his background, character, and work ethic were the exact traits that Coach Hughes looked for in a player. They were the traits that Coach Hughes would use as the architect of a great team. These traits would be the building blocks for his pursuit of excellence and putting a championship team on the floor.

While at Roberts, Stan proved to be more than just a basketball player. Stan not only earned a degree at Roberts, but in addition to playing basketball, he also achieved the following:

- Played four years of varsity soccer.
- Made the All-State team in varsity soccer.
- Was elected Class President his junior and senior years.
- Was named to Who's Who in American Colleges and Universities.
- Was inducted into the school's Athletic Hall of Fame for:
    o his own individual achievements and
    o his membership on the '65–'67 team.

Keith Moore, who played as the point guard and shooting guard during the '65-'67 championship years, recently attested to Stan's effectiveness, saying he could do it all. He was a catalyst for Coach Hughes in developing the half-court zone defense, a defense that really destroyed an opponent.

Keith mentioned something that we all knew about Stan. As good a ball handler as he was, he couldn't go left. He always went right. Opponents knew this, and even though they overplayed him on the right, he still beat them. He was uncanny. He was a very solid point guard, and I think if you were to get Coach Hughes to share who his best point guard was in all his years of coaching, he would tell you Stan Ziblut.

Stan loved Roberts Wesleyan and the people who attended there, and they loved him. The following quote was taken from Stan's recent written submission to the Raider Newsletter, a communication organ developed by the Hall of Fame team as a way of keeping in touch. I believe this quote articulates the essence of all sports.

> The effect on my life, having been a member of the '65–'66 basketball team, had little to do with wins and losses and everything to do with the friendships developed during my time with RWC basketball. The effect of the success

we shared loses some of its luster over time. The friendships developed became much more important and satisfying. (Stan Ziblut)

Role on the Team

Every team needs a player who can step up and take charge of executing the offensive and defensive game plans according to the wishes of the coach. He must be able to perform consistently and be stable and selfless. In doing so, he becomes a pillar of support for his teammates, freeing them up to do scoring, rebounding, assisting, or whatever they do well. The individual serves as a glue for the team, keeping the team together, focused, and poised. This person is often known as the floor general. On the '65–'66 Roberts Wesleyan team, the floor general was Stan Ziblut. Other terms could be substituted for floor general, such as point guard, but I think floor general fits Stan the best.

1965–1966 Cocaptains Stan Ziblut (24) and Frank Carter (40) and Head Coach Bill Hughes

CHAPTER 6

Rugged Players Emerge from the Heartland
Dale Easterly and Paul Crowell

The players on this team came from many different family backgrounds. Noel Smith's father was a police chief. Keith Moore's father was a minister. My father served as a recreation therapist at the Veteran's Administration. Some players like Frank Carter, Bill Bachmann, Stan Ziblut, and Keith Moore came from big cities. Others like Herman Schwingle, Ralph Roach, and Darwin Chapman came from small towns.

Western New York is the home of many farms. I am proud to say that two members of our team were raised on farms. This contributed to the team's diversity, a term that was not used a lot back then. I cannot speak to this myself, but I am told it takes an incredible work ethic, as well as a ceaseless sense of optimism, to make it as a farmer. Those two qualities are essential to success in sports as well. They were qualities that Coach Hughes valued greatly.

Paul Crowell was from Cherry Creek, New York, and Dale Easterly was from Chaffe which is near Arcade, New York. Paul and Dale were two of the most rugged, scrappy, and energetic players I ever played with.

Both players left an indelible mark on basketball at Roberts. They also won the respect of the student body with not only their athleticism but also their humility, their work ethic, and their Christian values. Sadly, we lost Dale Easterly in 2018 when he passed away from cancer.

Dale Easterly

Dale was recruited by Coach Hughes, who would readily admit that Dale was probably coming to Roberts anyway because of his Free Methodist background. But Coach Hughes loved Dale's scrappiness and ruggedness that I spoke of earlier and worked hard at recruiting Dale. Dale had the potential to make a significant contribution to athletics at Roberts.

When he arrived on campus, Dale turned potential into performances. Dale immediately made contributions to soccer and basketball. He was an outstanding defender in basketball who was often asked to guard the opposition's leading scorer. Blessed with long arms and legs, he was also the key "keeper" on the RWC soccer team for multiple seasons. In that capacity, Dale held several records, including career shutouts and season shutouts.

Often before basketball games, Coach Hughes would say, "Dale, you guard number 23 tonight." Number 23 might just as well go home because Dale would be all over him and not even allow him to get the ball. He was just that kind of defender.

Dale was also quite versatile, meaning that he could play the positions of shooting guard, point guard, and small forward. Whatever slot he was placed in, he adapted his skills to the position. A very quiet young man, Dale was very popular with his teammates. He used to wear black high-top "Chuck Taylor" sneakers, and he got the nickname "Jets," but how he got that moniker, I don't know.

It was not always an easy road for Dale. His work on the farm was vital to the farm's success. Sometimes, he had to ride a bike ten miles each way to get to practice. But he did it. It was a testament to Dale's character and commitment to the team. He was a four-year letterman on Arcade's basketball team, and he played in an era that was coined the "golden era" of Arcade basketball.

Summary of Dale's contribution and role on the team

Every team needs an all-around player who can start if necessary or come off the bench and spark the team. This player needs to perform consistently, be stable and selfless, and be willing to do what exactly the coach needs. He also needs to play stifling defense, often to shut down a hot hand on the opposition. These roles add up to one big role—defensive ace. On the '65–'67 Roberts Wesleyan team, Dale Easterly was that man. Dale just did his job well and with little fanfare. His role was to serve as the defensive ace on the team. He did not disappoint.

Paul Crowell

Paul Crowell came to Roberts in the fall of '65. He was a husky six feet four inches tall and had the body of a linebacker with the agility and speed to go with it. He was also as strong as an ox. In high school, Paul's skill development was steady, but it lagged behind his prodigious physical development. If he arrived at college today, coaches would say he has a lot of upside. What I am trying to say here is that he needed a little polish on his game like the rest of us. He was truly a "bull in a China shop."

Most players get more experienced and smarter every year, but they don't necessarily get better. Paul did. He was one of those rare athletes who got better every year. By his senior year in college, he was the leading scorer on the team, averaging twenty points per game. Not all players can say that, nor can they make that kind of leap. Paul and I probably played the most games together as teammates as compared to any other players in Roberts' history up to that point. We were the two leading scorers on the freshman team, and we played together all the way through to our senior year. I always loved playing with Paul. He backed down to no one. He was always there to back me up if the man I was guarding got around me and drove the lane (a situation which happened more than I would like to admit). When I would get the ball to him, one of three things would always happen, and they were all good.

1.   He would score.
2.   He would get fouled.
3.   He would put his opponent through the wall.

Of course, I am just kidding about the last one.

Paul had the misfortune of having to play behind some of the most talented and experienced big men in the school's history, which limited his playing time. But Paul still got into many games during the '66–'67 season, which was the last year of the team's championship run.

One of the greatest values that Paul brought to the team was his toughness in practice. This toughness kept the first team sharp (and a little sore, as Paul had no hesitancy in throwing some elbows around). I spoke to Noel Smith in February 2023 and asked him what it was like to go up against Paul every day in practice. Noel's reply, "It was rough, and I still have the bruises to prove it."

In high school, Paul was contacted by Roberts, and Roberts showed interest in his athletic ability. Paul knew all about Roberts as several family members had attended. From my personal point of view, Paul was a great teammate. I loved playing with him.

Role on the Team

Every team needs an enforcer—someone who can come off the bench and let the opposition know who is the boss. Starters go down with injuries, and good teams always have talent that can step in. Paul was perfect for this role. If one of our big guys was getting beat up or worn down in a physical game, Paul would be sent in to send a message. He was basically asked to soften up the opposition. During the championship season, Paul provided solid bench strength. He was placed in several tight game situations, and he held his own. He would have been a starter on 90 percent of the teams we played. Paul would have been classified as a power forward (4) or a center (5).

CHAPTER 7

Frank Carter and His Place in Roberts' History

Okay! I am going to say it now to get it out of the way. Frank Carter was the greatest player to ever put on a Basketball uniform at Roberts Wesleyan College—PERIOD. There are no ifs, ands, or buts about it. There, I said it. It needed to be said.

Wearing my writer's cap, I do not wish to be guilty of overstatement or hyperbole as I chronicle the exploits of my teammates on and off the court. However, when it comes to writing about Frank Carter, I do not know how I can avoid the appearance of amplification or embellishment in my writing as I attempt to describe Frank and his prodigious achievements during his basketball career. Frank Carter was, simply, as Coach Hughes stated at our team's Hall of Fame Induction Ceremony in 2017, a great, great player, one that rarely comes along.

I think I am uniquely qualified to make this statement as I have observed basketball at Roberts during the last fifty years. I have played on the Hall of Fame team, I have served as head basketball coach at Roberts, and I have attended hundreds of games as a fan. I have never seen a player at Roberts (during this fifty-year span) who had his skills and talents.

In addition to all this, he was also a nice guy. Everyone on campus loved him. He could have run for student body president and won hands down without doing any campaigning. He was voted by fellow students to be the king of winter weekend. His teammates loved him. On October 5, 2021, Keith Moore wrote a letter to the author in which he said, "Frank's death means that I have lost another hero. He was such a beautiful person and player. I felt complimented each time he passed me the ball." That statement says it all.

Frank passed away in 2021. Each surviving player wrote an entry into the electronic guestbook at the funeral home. As I read these poignant messages, one word constantly jumped off the pages, and that word was "privilege." Nearly all of his teammates said that it was not only a privilege to be on the court with him but also a privilege to be his friend. Everyone loved Frank Carter. Just as a rising tide lifts all boats, Frank lifted an entire campus with his other-worldly athletic skills and his irrepressible and ebullient personality.

How did a player like Frank get discovered and recruited by Roberts Wesleyan?

Much more needs to be said about Frank's place in the history of Roberts Wesleyan. Frank clearly had Division I talent and probably could have started for any school in the country. That includes Division 1 schools. So how did Coach Hughes find him and motivate him to enroll at the tiny school ten miles west of Rochester? It took time and patience. Here is the scoop.

At the time of Frank's recruitment, Coach Hughes was still new to the Western New York area. He readily admitted that he knew nothing about Niagara Falls and the fertile basketball recruiting ground that it spawned. However, in late 1962, Hughes received a call from an alumnus (considering what had transpired, this alumnus should be inducted into the Roberts Athletic Hall of Fame). Being an active member of the Free Methodist Church in Niagara Falls gave this alumnus much more credibility. Niagara Falls High School was awash with many good players. But this alumnus told Coach Hughes about Frank Carter. The Roberts alumnus knew what kind of kids would fit in at Roberts. Many kids from the Falls would not fit in at Roberts. Frank Carter would and did.

A Broken Leg Created a Huge Break
for Roberts Wesleyan

Frank's senior year in high school was the '62–'63 season, and during the Fall of 1962, Frank Carter was playing football. That is until he broke his leg badly. He would not be able to play basketball his senior year. Because of this, no opposing coaches could discover what a special talent he was. So Frank's loss was Roberts Wesleyan's opportunity. Even though he could not play during his high school year, his coach asked him to be on the bench every game. It was probably because of Frank's leadership ability and positive effect on players that the coach asked him to do this.

Coach Hughes set up a meeting with Frank and two of his teammates in the Niagara Falls school's guidance office. The two other players had major college potential. For some reason, the two other players left the meeting early, giving Coach Hughes more of an opportunity to focus on Frank. He asked Frank if he would like to visit the campus, and Frank said yes. Details were worked out for Frank to visit the weekend of the Eastern Regional, a big recruiting event for Roberts. Frank was escorted around campus by various members of the basketball team, and they must have done a good job because Frank Carter showed up in September, and a *new era of intercollegiate basketball was born at Roberts Wesleyan College.*

Frank Carter Earns All-American Honors

We know he is deserving of Little All-American honors. We just know he's that good. He can shoot, rebound, and play defense with the best of them. I've been in the Rochester areas for five years, and I've never seen a college player who was better."

The speaker was Roberts Wesleyan basketball coach Bill Hughes, and the subject was Roberts Wesleyan basketball star Frank Carter. The coach's prediction was right on the money, as Frank Carter was named an NAIA small college ALL-AMERICAN at the end of the season. There were six hundred teams in the NAIA (which stands for National Association of Intercollegiate Athletics) back then, meaning there were over six thousand players competing. At the end of the year, the top twenty-five players were selected for First Team All-American honors. The next fifteen players were selected for honorable mention. Frank Carter was in that group.

Carter Becomes All-Time Leading Scorer

From December 9, 1966, *Democrat and Chronicle*—Frank Carter, the finest basketball player in Roberts Wesleyan history and a candidate for small college All-American honors, will take dead aim tonight on the only major school record that he does not already own.

When Carter and his teammates take the floor on the Churchville-Chili court against the University of Toronto, Carter will be only 31 points behind the all-time Roberts Wesleyan career scoring record of 1,453. The record was held by Garth Stam and was set in 1953. While it took Stam seventy-six games to set the standard, Carter will have taken only sixty-five if he hits more than 31 tonight. Frank needed 31 to tie the record and 32 to break the record. He scored 32.

Carter receives game ball from Coach Hughes.

CHAPTER 8

A Rebounding Machine
Bill Bachmann

I must tell it like it is. *Bill Bachmann was the best rebounder in the history of basketball at Roberts Wesleyan College—period.* Fifty years later, he still holds the rebounding record for rebounds per game. He was a great, great rebounder. If you need proof, just ask Bill. Sadly, we lost Bill in 2017 to pancreatic cancer.

An illustration of his rebounding intensity can be seen in the famous Buffalo State game. I entered the game in the first half and grabbed a loose ball near half-court. I headed down the court with what looked to be a wide-open layup. However, out of nowhere, three Buff State players were on my tail, and they were fast. If I went for a conventional layup, there was a good chance one of the Buff State guys would reach over my back and block it. What was once a promising scoring opportunity now was looking dubious. Instead of doing a conventional layup, I faked by bringing the ball up and then bringing the ball down by my knees and scooping it up to the basket. I missed the shot, and the crowd groaned. But wait. Out of nowhere, Bill Bachmann entered the picture, rebounded my miss, and put it in while getting fouled—a three-point play. Thrilled that I was off the hook, I started to realize why Bill was such a great rebounder.

He wanted the ball more than anyone on the court!

Breaking the play down further, let's look at where Bill was when I got that loose ball at half-court. He was down on the low post guarding Charlie Davis. He was further away from our basket than anyone on the court. He had to outrun all the players on both teams to make the play, and he did. He was there to get the rebound and score. Our forwards and guards were closer to the action, but they did not get to the play—Bill Bachmann did. Bill wanted credit on the stat sheet for as many rebounds as possible. While that may seem selfish, his rebound work was actually a stimulus to all of us to start the fast break and go down and score.

Rebounding is not glamorous. However, it is critical to success in basketball. A lot of successful rebounding is guts, desire, hard work, and positioning. Bill Bachmann had all those qualities. Bill Bachmann was blessed with a wiry 6–5 body and lots of athleticism. But what vaulted him to becoming one of the top rebounders in the country was his intense desire to win and, at the same time, fill up the stat sheet. His competitive zeal rubbed off on all of us and made us a better team. In some ways, Bill was like the soul of the team. He always led the banter in the locker room. Once before, a preseason practice, he yelled out to Noel Smith, "Hey, Noel, how's my man doing?" Noel, being a very independent young man with a great sense of humor, had a quick retort, which was funny. Unfortunately, I cannot remember his exact words. Noel's response did not affect Bill at all. Bill acted like he was in pain, but he laughed it off and went off to find someone else to hassle.

Bill loved the team until the day he died, which was in late September 2017. Ten days earlier, despite being in unbearable pain from pancreatic cancer, which he had for two years, he made the trip from his home in Florida to the campus of Roberts Wesleyan to participate in ceremonies for the team's induction to the Roberts Athletic Hall of Fame. He received two standing ovations from the assembled crowd.

Our championship team has had many reunions over the years, and Bill Bachmann took charge of organizing and promoting all these affairs. Bill had a big heart, and he even funded the flight for a former administrator who loved this team but had fallen into financial difficulties.

Bill came out of Penn Hills High School in Pittsburg, Pennsylvania, where he played basketball and baseball. He was pretty raw, and I have no evidence that he was highly recruited. He was involved with a youth group at his local Free Methodist Church. Back in the '60s, the Western Pennsylvania Free Methodist Churches supplied Roberts with many fine students, including Bill Bachmann.

Let's be honest; Bill had an ego. As teammates, we kept him humble. The following anecdote is revealing. During the first Chase-Lincoln Tournament, things were close in the second half. RIT was playing a 2–3 zone defense. I was directing the play from the point. An RIT player got out of position, and suddenly, Bill was wide open underneath. I fired the ball at him, knowing that the pass would have to navigate through many waving arms. As soon as the pass left my hand, I said to myself, "I threw it too hard. He'll never catch it. It's too hard." But Bill caught it and put it in for two points. After the game, I went up to him and said, "Bill, thanks for catching that pass. I threw it way too hard." He looked at me, and with a straight face, he said, "Scribs, my boy (he always called me his boy), always remember one thing. If it means two points for Bachmann, I'll catch anything."

Bachmann wins MVP trophy at Chase
Tournament in Rochester, New York.
Coach Hughe's son holds the basketball.

CHAPTER 9

Sectional MVP
Ralph Roach

Not many members of the greatest team in Roberts' history won a sectional title in their high school careers. The exception was Keith Moore, who was on a team that won the State title in Maryland. Even fewer Roberts players (if there were any) were named MVP in their sectional tourneys—no one, that is, except Ralph Roach. Ralph was named MVP of the Section 5 Sectionals in 1966, scoring 30 points in one of the games. He played at Hilton High School, a few miles west of Rochester. It was the *last* Sectional title won by Hilton until this very day—fifty-seven years.

Ralph came to Roberts in the Fall of '66. Coach Hughes recruited him persistently. Because Ralph was a guard, he was a threat to my position on the team, and I knew I would have to take care of business. This coming year was to be my first full year on the varsity, and I was not about to relinquish my potential spot to a freshman, even if he led his high school to a sectional championship. In a way, that was a good thing. Ralph's presence made me a better player. I have to say that Ralph never acted like he wanted my spot. He just played hard. It was sort of a break for me that Ralph played soccer because the seasons overlapped, and he got a late start in basketball. Coach Hughes also seemed to be loyal to players who thoroughly knew his system, and I was one of those players. The bottom line was that Ralph started the season on the freshman team coached by Harry Hutt.

Ralph performed so well on the Freshman team that he was brought up to the varsity after five games. Harry Hutt said, in his humorous way, that he coached Ralph just long enough to mess him up. Ralph had tremendous respect for the players ahead of him on the varsity team. He was sort of buried deep on the varsity bench, but I don't think it bothered him because he recognized the excellence of the players ahead of him. Ralph, in an interview with the author on March 28, 2023, said he got an education from practicing on a daily basis with all of these great players. He knew his time would come. Plus, he got in a lot of games because we were always so far ahead, and the bench subs often had a chance to play.

Now that raises a good point. I have said several times that this team was unselfish and dedicated to team play. After being such a star in high school, it would have been easy for Ralph to sulk or have an attitude; he didn't. His attitude was very positive, and he won the respect of his teammates. The difference between the fifth-best player and the ninth-best player on the team was razor-thin. It was no dishonor to not start. Coach Hughes often said that most of the second-stringers would have started for the opposition.

Ralph played for four years at Roberts. He had a solid career. I was a starter in my junior year.

The thing that always impressed me about him was his uncanny ability to draw fouls and get to the foul line. I saw games where he would score 18 points and have only two field goals.

Being a two-sport athlete, Ralph made such a great contribution to Roberts' athletics that he was named to the Roberts Athletic Hall of Fame.

CHAPTER 10

The PhDs
Darwin Chapman and Glen Shultz

The members of this team were no slouches when it came to academics. I do not have the actual records, but I would surmise that the average GPA on the team was higher than the average GPA on campus. Two of our teammates, Glen Schultz and Darwin Chapman, as well as our manager, Paul Mroz, went on to distinguish themselves by earning PhDs. We are all proud of their achievements.

Dr. Darwin Chapman

Darwin earned his PhD in speech pathology. The '66–'67 season was the only season that Darwin played, and what a great year he chose to participate. It was the best year in Roberts' history. Like many of his teammates, Darwin grew up in a small town, Akron, New York. While attending Akron Central School, Darwin started on the varsity team his senior year. At Roberts, he played on the freshman team his first year, and in his sophomore year, he made it to the varsity team, no small feat when considering all the talented players on the team. He was a very hard worker and well-respected by his teammates. During practices, he pushed the starters hard and made the team stronger. The following year, his junior year, he planned a course of action that not many athletes make. He decided to focus on getting into the best graduate school in the field of speech pathology, and in doing so, he had to put basketball behind him. After finishing his degree, he became a practicing speech pathologist and taught at several major universities.

Dr. Glen Schultz

The chapter heading for Glen Schultz could have easily been "from one-room schoolhouse to the Roberts Hall of Fame." Glen actually attended a one-room schoolhouse in the school system that later became known as Starpoint Central School.

He started playing basketball in sixth grade. He did well in the sport and continued playing through high school, where he was a two-year starter. He became known as an outstanding defensive player, and he was always assigned to guard the best player on the opposing team. Glen also ran on the cross-country team in high school.

His Dad went to Roberts, and Glen was ready to follow his father. Coach Hughes was aware of Glen but did not vigorously pursue him, probably because it was a done deal that Glen was coming to Roberts Wesleyan College.

The pressbook at Roberts stated that he was the scrappiest player on the team. I remember that, except for Frank Carter, Glen was the only teammate I ever saw dunk in a game. Keith Moore stated that Glen was one of the most dependable players on the team, adding that he always seemed to be in the right place at the right time.

Glen averaged 4.2 points per game and 3.2 rebounds per game in '65–'66 and 9.2 points per game and 6.4 rebounds per game for the '66–'67 team. He was clearly a major contributor to both great teams.

Glen was a leader, and it was no surprise that he was voted a cocaptain for the '67–'68 team. Like Stan Ziblut, Glen distinguished himself in activities other than basketball. He was named king of winter weekend his senior year, and he was elected to Who's Who in American colleges and universities. He was inducted into the Roberts Wesleyan Athletic Hall of Fame in 2003.

Having grown up in a Christian home, Glen received his doctorate degree in education and has become a leader in the field of Christian education. He is the author of two books.

CHAPTER 11

Paul Mroz Ph.D.
Team Manager

The job of team manager is one of the most thankless jobs in all sports. The manager is responsible for gathering all the sweaty uniforms after a game, laundering them, and handing them out to individual players at the next game. Other duties include gathering and safeguarding all the team's valuables during a game, supervising the people keeping stats, keeping stats himself, and being always available to the coach. There was no pay.

Our team was blessed to have Dr. Paul Mroz (class of '69) serve as team manager during our triumphant run. Paul was very well-liked by all the players, and he did a good job. Paul grew up on a small farm in Corfu, New York, and he brought the farmer's work ethic with him to college. He was always ready to do anything to help another person.

Paul was very successful in his career as a science teacher. He taught biology, chemistry, and physics at the high school level. He coached on several different levels in the Spencerport Central Schools in Spencerport, NY where he compiled impressive win-loss records in soccer year after year. He somehow found time to go back to school and earn a doctorate in meteorology. Using that degree, he became a weekend meteorologist for WOKR TV in Rochester. He was also on the faculty at SUNY Brockport and Roberts Wesleyan College.

Meet the Coach
Bill Hughes

Head Coach Bill Hughes

CHAPTER 12

The Coach
Bill Hughes

Coach Hughes

Up to this point, I have shared with you information about my teammates, where they came from, and their basketball histories. We have learned how they found their way to Roberts and how they performed when they arrived there. It is one thing to recruit and assemble talent. It is another thing to get that talent to play together. Some very talented teams never live up to the hype that precedes them. A poor coach can destroy a good team by over-coaching or any other of many possible bad moves.

From the mid-1950s to the early 1960s, the basketball program at Roberts was somewhat adrift, which may be putting it mildly. The team's record from the '54–'55 season to the '60–'61 season was 45–85. The players were morphing into playground soloists, and there was a lack of team discipline and team play. It was time for new leadership.

Dr. Ellwood Voller became the President of the college in 1957. As a former coach himself, it was his job to hire and fire the division and departmental leaders at the college. If Dr. Voller were to write up a job description for a new coach needed at that time, it probably would have looked like this:

- A disciplinarian who had a firm hand at the helm who could keep the team focused.
- A visionary who could challenge individual players and the team as a whole to achieve and to go places that had never entered their minds.
- A solid game manager who could:
  a) Set up the perfect out-of-bounds play with five seconds on the clock and the game tied and
  b) who could make the right substitutions at the right times.
- A creative strategist who could chart the course for the future as well as size up the next opponent and exploit their weaknesses
- A person with good PR skills who could:
  a) Passionately promote the team and the college in various communities.
  b) Speak effectively at alumni functions.
  c) Be a partner (when called upon) in fund-raising and college relations.
- A principled person who could lead by example and teach the great lessons of life to a group of young men; a person who could live and teach Christian values.

There was a man out there who was the perfect man for this job. He met all the criteria. His name was William Virgil Hughes, and he was known to all of us players as Coach. (Note: I have so much respect for Coach Hughes that I still cannot call him by his everyday name, Bill. Nor do I desire to do so. He will always be my coach.)

Coach Hughes had a strong personality, and he was full of ideas and ideals. His desire to win was as wide as the Texas sky under which he was born. His demeanor could be categorized by the three Cs:

- Charismatic,
- Confident, and
- Controversial

Charismatic. Let's be straightforward. Coach Hughes was a sharp-looking guy. Plus, his wardrobe looked like it was out of *Gentleman's Quarterly*. His speech was characterized by a slight Midwestern accent, and he had a deep, rich voice. He was a very good speaker, and he always used basketball stats to show how his team was improving. When he spoke, people listened. He commanded the attention of the audience. The man exuded charisma. He knew how to work a room.

Confident. Coach Hughes approached everything he did with confidence. If it was a game he was coaching, he was always extremely confident that if his advice was followed, there was no question about who would win. The confidence also came through in his body language. He always looked people in the eyes as he spoke. His gaze was powerful. If a person were to ask him for something, that person better have the facts straight.

Controversial. Coach was never afraid to take a stand. He lived his life and coached his teams according to a set of principles and values in which he deeply believed. He expected his players to adopt these values. If a player challenged his values, there would be a price to pay, and it would not be paid by the coach. Some saw this stance on his part as rigid and inflexible.

Longevity for rebellious players was brief. Those who remained quickly realized the coach's wisdom. Some players rebelled. They did not last long. In the long run, the players came to see that the coach was right. The players whom he recruited later in his tenure respected him greatly for his adherence to principle.

How Did Coach Hughes Get to Roberts?

His journey began in high school when he and three of his buddies (who became life-long friends) decided to enroll in Central College in Kansas, a Free Methodist College, for their senior year. Central College had a high school at that time. Surprisingly, high school students were able to participate in the college athletic teams, and the young Bill Hughes took advantage of this. He ended up playing for three years at Central and started every year. Upon graduating from Central he went on to Greenville College in Illinois for his Junior and Senior years. The basketball team was very strong at Greenville at that time, but he won a spot in the varsity and became a valuable reserve.

Coach Hughes recently stated in the Raider Gazette![2] That he had three years of living the role Gene Hackman played in the movie *Hoosiers*, as he cut his coaching teeth as head coach in two different Illinois High Schools in one of the most fanatical basketball areas in the entire state. He was actually fired from his first job because he pushed the boys too hard. Wow!

He held on to his second job for two years, and then President Voller called him and asked him to interview for the coaching job at Roberts. He must have been impressive because he was offered the head basketball coaching job as well as the athletic director position. As the coach remembers, Dr. Voller was very clear that he wanted a disciplined, winning program with an emphasis on the discipline part.

During his high school and college careers, Bill Hughes played for seven different coaches. He took ideas on basketball and coaching from each of them, and he began to develop his own philosophy. However, there was a slight roadblock for Roberts to find Hughes. Roberts Wesleyan was in Rochester, New York, and Coach Hughes was in Illinois. How would they find each other? Wherever there is

---

[2] The Raider Gazette was also known as the Raider Newsletter. It was a communication organ designed to keep the team in touch with each other. The players submitted articles, and those articles made up the body of the publications. Only two volumes were produced, one in 2022 and one in 2023.

a will, there's a way. Dr. Voller was good friends with Clark Snyder, who was on the Roberts' Board of Trustees. The Snyder family highly recommended Bill Hughes for the job.

They learned of Bill Hughes when Bill got engaged to their daughter Shirley while at Greenville. Dr. Voller flew Hughes to Rochester for an interview. Coach Hughes got the job and, all at once, became the athletic director, physical education director, head soccer coach, and head basketball coach at Roberts Wesleyan College.

The journey taken by Bill Hughes to Roberts included some interesting side trips. To be complete with this depiction, we must answer how he got to Central and Greenville Colleges. However, the quality that, I believe, enabled Coach Hughes to stand out as a coach surfaced, not when he was playing basketball as a youth, but when he was running track. Let me explain how I uncovered this. On January 3, 2023, I interviewed Coach Hughes over the phone. He was in Dallas, and I was in Rochester, New York.

As I asked him to take me through his athletic experiences as a youth, I was looking for something that would give me a clue about what it was that made him tick. He told me how he did not make the junior high basketball team yet became good enough to make the varsity a few years later and then play on one of the best high school teams in Dallas. That was impressive, but it still did not give me the clue I was looking for.

He told me how, while in high school, he became a good sprinter on track, not the fastest, but fast.

He went on to explain how he was always picked to anchor the relay teams. I asked him why they picked him if he wasn't the fastest. I will never forget his reply.

"They picked me because I had a lot of guts."

A lot of guts. Right then, I knew what exactly he meant, and I knew I had uncovered the essence of what made him an outstanding coach. It became more and more obvious.

The man hated to lose.

His track coach knew it and knew that his desire to win trumped raw talent. As one who played for him, I think back, and it is so obvious. This guy was a great coach because he hated to lose.

Because he hated to lose, he did more of the little things that were necessary to win. He would drive hundreds of miles to scout a team we were playing in the next week. He worked on the small things in practice that could be big things in a game, like being able to execute our stall offense or practice our offense against a 1-2-2 full-court press.

Six Characteristics That All Players Want to See in Their Coach

What do players want from a coach? I believe that players have very strong opinions about how their coach should behave and lead as a coach. If a coach embodies those proper characteristics, there will be more buy-in from the players. If the coach lacks any of these qualities, his/her chances of success diminish.

A good coach is always so central to success. A coach, by the very nature of his/her position, creates an atmosphere in which the team lives throughout the season. This atmosphere can be extremely positive, extremely negative, or somewhere in between. Based on my experience playing for several different coaches, the following behaviors are crucial to coaching success and establishing the proper atmosphere:

- A strong, intense desire to win.
- Able to set challenging goals for the team.
- Belief in players.
- Ability to be firm yet fair.
- A strong work ethic.
- Ability to demand and get the best out of each player.

A young coach may not possess all these qualities at the beginning of his/her career but can develop them over time. I believe that Coach Hughes embodied all these qualities. There was no question about his desire to win. Players could see it in his actions, his preparation, his scouting, and his overall approach to the game.

When it came to setting challenging goals, there was no question that Coach Hughes did this. At the first practice in the fall of 1965, he came right out and stated that our goal was to make it to the national championship tournament in Kansas City. I did not know Coach at the time, but at that point, I decided that I liked this guy. This was momentous stuff for a guy like me coming out of Batavia, New York, where perhaps my teams at the YMCA ventured a few miles down the road to play a game. Kansas City seemed so grand, and I decided that I definitely wanted to be a part of it.

In terms of believing in his players, I can only speak for myself. Having never played high school ball, I was pretty nervous in my first couple of games. In the first game of the '66–'67 season against Bethel College, he put me in during the first half, and being quite nervous, I turned the ball over a couple of times. He yanked me right out, and as I was headed to the bench, I figured that my career was over. I was so discouraged. But about five minutes later, he put me right back in the game, and I did fine. The message I received was that he believed in me. That meant so much to me.

Coach Hughes was very firm but also fair. He disciplined the starters of the team just as he disciplined the others. No one got any special treatment, as Bill Bachmann can attest.

There was no question about his work ethic. He put in long hours.

He also brought out the best in each of us. I never played as hard for any other coaches as I played for Coach Hughes. I did not dare give less than 100 percent. If I did, he would see it and call me on it.

A Look Back

Before going any further, I ask you to take a look at what you are about to learn. We have comments and data on players dating back sixty years. And we can compare those comments from sixty years ago to comments the same players made today. I doubt that most books on sports today can make this claim.

Near the end of the book, I (Dave) will share these very special thoughts with you. These questions were posed to the players in late 2022, *fifty-five years after they finished their careers*. Their answers were poignant and compelling. You will see the responses in a later chapter. Each player was asked the following questions:

- How did being a member of this team affect your life?
    - o Your outlook on life?
    - o What effect did the experience have on your career?
    - o Your self-confidence?
- Pick the experience or event that had the greatest impact on you or was the most meaningful to you. Describe the experience with as much detail as possible and describe your reaction.
- If a current or future student was doing research on the history of athletics at Roberts Wesleyan, what would you want that student to know about this team?

CHAPTER 13

The 1965–66 Games

Stalled Out in Indiana

I was a freshman during the '65–'66 season. About forty guys went out for the team that year. Coach Hughes whittled the team down to twelve players, of which I was one. He stated that only ten would make the team. I desperately wanted to make the top ten. I did not. But looking at what transpired, I probably benefitted more by being on the freshman team because I got a lot more playing time. If I had been on varsity, I would have spent a lot of time on the bench.

The first three games of the '65–'66 season were in Winona Lake, Indiana, where we played in the Grace College Tournament. I felt sad as I watched the bus pull out of the Roberts parking lot. I really wanted to be on that bus.

There were eight teams in the tournament, all Christian Colleges from the Midwest. In our first game of the year, we beat Bethel College of Mishawaka, Indiana, 94–90. The next day, we beat Grace College, 83–81. Our third game was against Malone College of Ohio, and we were upset by Malone, 55–53. The fact that the three games we played were decided by a total of 8 points indicates how well-balanced this tournament was.

Malone knew they could not get into a fast-paced game with us, so they slowed the game down. We had a lead deep into the second half, and we went into a stall offense to protect the lead. We did not execute it well, and Malone caught us and nipped us at the last minute. The outcome was difficult to accept.

Frank Carter was named Most Valuable Player in the tournament. Bill Bachmann was selected to the all-tournament team.

Record 2–1
Gaining Momentum in Defeating Two State Schools

After returning from Indiana, the Raiders took on the Knights of Geneseo State at Geneseo. We were taking on a team that we had defeated in twenty-five of the last thirty-two games. We beat Geneseo 96–84. It was the start of what proved to be the longest winning streak in the history of Raider basketball. It was a close game until Roberts launched its formidable half-court press in the second half. We got a lot of steals and pulled away for the win.

A couple of days later, we took on the Lakers of Oswego State at Oswego, the defending State University of New York champs. The Lakers had won six of the last seven games against us, and they had a strong team. We squeaked out a 65–62 win.

I scored 20 for the freshman team against Geneseo, and I pumped in 21 against Oswego. I was always anxious to get showered after the freshman game and get out into the gymnasium to watch the varsity warm-up. It was a real show. I also closely watched our varsity players, particularly Stan Ziblut and Keith Moore, who teamed up at the guard position where I knew I would be playing the following year.

Record 4–1
A Winning Streak Is Emerging

Next up was Eastern Nazarene, whom we took on at home. We came away with a 91–78 win. Eastern Nazarene did not have a Freshman team, so we played a team called the U of R Medics. I scored 23 points, and all of a sudden, I was leading the freshman team in scoring.

We then faced off with Brockport State. Brockport was a physical education school, and located near Roberts, so there was sort of a natural rivalry. Brockport had over three thousand students as compared to eight hundred at Roberts. We unceremoniously disposed of the Golden Eagles, 73–55. I was invited by Coach Hughes to warm up with the varsity and sit on the bench. I was thrilled. I also poured in 19 against the Brockport Frosh.

Next up was Alfred University. We defeated the Saxons, 98–71. Frank Carter scored 37 points. Bachmann and Moore added 18 and 15 points respectively. It was our fifth straight victory, and we started to take aim at the school record for consecutive wins, which was eight. During all those wins, Frank Carter established himself as a superstar, and Bill Bachmann cleaned off the boards. I scored 18 against the Alfred freshmen.

Record 7–1
North of the Border

Our next two games were in Canada, where we took on McMaster University and the University of Toronto. Coach Hughes brought me along to get some varsity seasoning, and I played during garbage time in each game. It was a great experience. And I liked the attention I was getting from Coach Hughes.

We disposed of McMaster University, 68–55 and broke the century mark against Toronto, scoring 111 points against their 86. We came up two points short of tying the school team record of 113 points set in the '64–'65 season.

Record 9–1
Carter Sets School Record for Points in a Game

On January 15, Roberts hosted a very good Oneonta State team and the game turned out to be one of the most memorable games in Roberts' history. Frank Carter, hitting shots from all over the court, scored 54 points to set a new single-game scoring record. He broke the record of 50 set by Ken Lescalleet.

Roberts totally dominated throughout the game. At one point during the first half, I looked at the scoreboard, and the score was 46–8 Roberts. But it was Frank's night. Sitting and watching him, I marveled at what a great athlete he was. There can be real beauty in human movement. Frank modeled that beauty. His jump shot was so pure. His wrists flicked perfectly on the release. His thunderous dunks were so smooth and explosive. During his four years at Roberts, we were all privileged to see a rare talent. In case you are interested, I had 15 in the preliminary game against a school known as RBI, which stands for Rochester Business Institute.

Record 10–1
Ithaca College

The Raiders journeyed to Ithaca College for what turned into a closely fought game. Behind much of the game, Roberts scored the winning basket just before the buzzer sounded to prevail '69–'68. This marked the ninth straight win for the team, breaking the record of eight in a row during the '64–'65 season.

Record 11–1

The next two weeks saw the Raiders win four in a row. Brockport, Geneseo, Fredonia, and St. John Fisher were all defeated by the Raider juggernaut. The winning streak went up to 13 games, an all-time school record.

Record 15–1
Buffalo State Becomes a Bump in the
Road as the Winning Streak Ends

On February 12, Roberts traveled to Buffalo to take on a top opponent, Buffalo State. Roberts had never beaten Buffalo State in seven earlier encounters. Buffalo was one of the elite basketball programs in the Northeast, and they were an attractive opponent because they provided a good measuring stick for us to gauge how good we were.

It was a closely fought game. Buffalo led by a small margin for most of the game. Roberts fell behind by 10 points late in the game before staging a gutsy rally which got them to within 4 points. That was as close as they could get, and they lost 67–63.

Thus, the winning streak was over. But as many people say, records are made to be broken, so please keep reading. You will learn the role Buffalo State played in another winning streak in the next chapter.

Record 15–2
Raiders Continue to Dominate Rochester Competition

The team got back in the groove against two longtime local opponents, St. John Fisher and RIT.

Against Fisher, the Raiders cracked the century mark, winning 102 to 72 on the Fisher court. The next game was against powerful RIT. Roberts trailed by two at the half. Believe me, things were not pleasant in the locker room at halftime. Employing their vaunted half-court press during most of the second half, the Raiders turned the game around and went on to win by a score of 92 to 86.

In recent years, Roberts no longer has scheduled games with local college teams. There are probably many reasons for this, but I believe that this is a mistake. Fans would enjoy it.

Record 17–2
The Regular Season Winds Down

(The next paragraph is taken from the 1965–66 Chesbronian.)

In the Eastern Baptist Invitational, the Raiders chalked up an impressive victory against Lincoln University. The following night saw the Raiders play one of the toughest teams in District 31 of the NAIA. The game went right down to the wire and saw the Raiders fall short by only one point as they were defeated by Trenton State of New Jersey by a score of 79–78. Frank Carter was selected as the

53

most valuable player in the tourney, and Bill Bachmann was selected for the All-Tournament Team (1965–66 Chesbronian; page 159).

Record 18–3

"On Wednesday, February 22, after winning more games than any previous team in the school's history, the Raiders accepted a bid to the District 31 NAIA playoffs. Thus, for the first time in the history of Roberts Wesleyan College athletics, the basketball team represented the college in a post-season tournament, a fitting tribute to a deserving group of athletes" (1965–66 Chesbronian, page 159).

NAIA District Playoff

We drew a very tough team in the NAIA District playoff, Monmouth College of New Jersey. Monmouth defeated us 75–63. They went to Kansas City for the National tournament. We stayed home and licked our wounds as we said goodbye to seniors Stan Ziblut, Herm Schwingle, and Bob Ahlin.

It was a great season for the Raiders.

CHAPTER 14

The 1966–67 Team

The school's yearbook, known as the *Chesbronian,* said it best, and I quote:

"Basketball 'fever' again was present as this year's varsity emerged to break all the records of the previous year and become the greatest team in Roberts' history. With a big, exciting team to cheer on, the RWC fans kept pace all year with their loyal support. The varsity finished with a 20–3 record, 20–5 overall, including the post-season playoffs."

There is no sense arguing which team was better; was it the '65–'66 team or the '66–'67 team? Each team only lost three regular season games. Each team set a record for wins in a season. Each team was outstanding.

I will say that the '66–'67 team experienced three watershed events that will live in the memories of fans and players forever.

- First was the Buffalo State game, where we beat a great Buff State team, which was the best small college team in the Northeast. It was our sixteenth straight win played in front of a standing-room-only crowd at Churchville-Chili High School. Many fans never got in because the Fire Marshalls started closing the doors two hours before game time. It was the first time Roberts had ever beaten Buff Stat. You will read about this game later.

- Second was winning the inaugural Monroe Country Collegiate championship (and we didn't know it at the time), which became the longest-running collegiate in-season tournament in the country. We beat St. John Fisher in the finals, led by the late Bill Bachmann, who was named the tournament's most valuable player. This tournament really showcased our team to the Rochester community.

- The third event occurred as we were coming home from eastern Pennsylvania, where we lost a heartbreaker in overtime in the NAIA playoffs. I will never forget the sight of our team bus approaching the intersection of Orchard Street and Buffalo Road in North Chili. There were police cars stopping traffic, and I saw hundreds of students, faculty, staff, and community members lining the streets as they cheered and welcomed us home. This was followed by an enthusiastic pep rally in the dining hall. As Coach Hughes said in his speech during the Hall of Fame induction ceremony, "Seeing all people rallying around us, the whole experience was like a fairy-tale." You will also read more about this event later in the book.

Another Hiccup in Hoosier Land

For the second year in a row, we opened the season in Winona Lake, Indiana, at the Grace College tournament. Only Christian colleges were invited to participate. Most of these schools were from the Midwest, and these guys could all play. The participating teams included the following colleges: Goshen, Grace, Huntington, Bethel, Spring Arbor, Tri-State, and Trinity. We fully expected to win the tournament. We didn't.

We ran into a stubborn, resilient bulldog team from Mishawaka, Indiana, known as Bethel College. They showed us no fear or respect. We just couldn't pull away from them. They beat us 97–92. How could this have happened? We thought we could go undefeated, and we lost our first game. We were feeling so low that we could have hung ourselves from a curb.

I contributed nothing. I played so poorly in the first half that I thought Coach Hughes would bench me for the rest of the year, except for a couple of mop-up roles in Canada the previous year, this was technically my first varsity game, and I was nervous and tight. But Coach put me in during the second half, and I did much better. He must have had faith in me because he started me in the next game.

Record 0–1

In the second game of the tournament, we played Trinity College. I started, and to this day, I do not know why. I hit my first two shots, and I was off and running. I knew I would be an integral part of the team. We defeated Trinity, 93–73. This win was significant because it was the start of a record-breaking sixteen-game winning streak.

Record 1–1

In the third game, we rolled over Huntington College, 93–81. Significant in the win was the fact that we scored over 90 points in the game. This prolific scoring would continue throughout the season, and we ended the year averaging 91 points per game—a school record. To put this into perspective, the 2021–22 Gonzaga team led all major colleges in the nation in team scoring, but with only 85 points per game.

I had four points in that game, and my confidence was building. We were disappointed with our loss in Indiana, but we learned a great deal from it. We learned that we were capable of losing and that to achieve our goals, we needed to be fully focused in every game.

Record 2–1

Our next game was a home game against a powerful Detroit college team. We ran past this team from the motor city by a score of 124–105. The 124 points constituted a new team record for points in a game, breaking the old record of 113 set two years earlier against Eastern Nazarene. I think Coach Hughes was glad that we won, but he was not very happy that we gave up 105 points. Frank Carter showed off his many gifts on his way to scoring 42 points.

Record 3–1
Roberts Slams Brockport

The headline in the *Democrat and Chronicle* read, "Carter Paces Roberts Rout of Brockport." We dominated our Westside neighbors by a score of 101–55. Frank Carter had 32 points to lead the way. Five Raider players hit double figures. At that point in the season, we were averaging 101 points per game while holding the opposition to less than 80. Roberts led by five points at halftime. Our zone press enabled us to limit Brockport to 22 points in the second half as we ran to a forty-six-point victory. During one stretch in the second half, we outscored Brockport 27–2. This, as you will see, became a pattern for our games. We would allow the opposition to remain close to us, and then Coach Hughes would unleash either a half-court or full-court press, and we would go on a run that usually knocked the opponent out of the game. On a personal note, I scored 14 points in this game, my highest total of the year.

Record 4–1
Carter Becomes All-Time Career Scoring
Leader against University of Toronto

I quote an article in the *Democrat and Chronicle*, "red hot Roberts Wesleyan College whipped the University of Toronto 123 to 78 last night at Churchville-Chili high school. Frank Carter, Roberts' six-foot-two candidate for little All-American honors, scored 32 points to set a new Roberts career scoring record. Carter, from Niagara Falls, is averaging slightly more than 31 points per game. He broke Garth Stam's record with two minutes and fifty-three seconds remaining and has now scored 1454 points in sixty-five games, eclipsing the old mark of 1453 in seventy-six games by Garth Stam in 1953."

Record 5–1
Roberts Routs Fisher

Despite falling below its 100 points per game average, Roberts defeated St. John Fisher by 32 points at the Cardinals' home court. Frank Carter contributed 25 points to pace the Raiders. Keith Moore and Dale Easterly scored 18 and 14 points, respectively.

Record 6–1
Curtis Nets 30 as Roberts Races
to Seventh Straight Win

Roberts easily defeated Fredonia State 94–62, with Ken Curtis leading the way with 30 points. Trailing at halftime, the Raiders surged ahead as they went on a 32–7 run in the second half. Curtis was recruited from John Marshall High School in Rochester, where he was one of the leading scorers and rebounders in the Rochester City-Catholic League. He was projected to become a great scorer at Roberts. He showed us all about what was to come.

Record 7–1
Roberts Clips Oswego for Eighth Win in a Row

"Tonight's game marks the eighth game in this series between the two colleges. The Lakers have completely dominated this series, winning six of the past seven games. Robert scored its first victory over Oswego last year by a score of 65–62. In the first eight games, Frank Carter continues to scorch the nets, shooting 51 percent from the field and averaging 30.1 points a game. The team is averaging 103 points per game with an average winning margin of 25 points per game."

The *Democrat and Chronicle* reported that Roberts looked sluggish as they squandered a 15-point lead in the second half, allowing the Lakers to get within 5 points before pulling away.

Record 8–1
Roberts Tops Geneseo State for Ninth Straight Win

This game marked the twenty-first meeting between the Knights of Geneseo and the Raiders. The Knights won 8 games and the Raiders 12. In this game, Geneseo led 40–35 at the half. With ten minutes left in the game, the Raiders rallied and went on a 17–0 run to put the game away. Roberts defeated Geneseo 95–80 for their ninth win in a row.

Record 9–1
Roberts Tops Oneonta for Tenth in a Row

The following is taken from a special to the *Democratic and Chronicle*. "In a game at Oneonta, high-flying Roberts Wesleyan, spurred by Frank Carter and Bill Bachmann, rolled to its tenth consecutive victory against Oneonta State tonight by a score of 102–77. Frank Carter again led the way with 27 points."

An interesting memory for me was the fact that the team was invited to the local Free Methodist Church the next morning (Sunday) to participate in the service. I remember watching Coach Hughes sing in a quartet with some of my teammates. Noel Smith and Ken Curtis took up the collection. Also we were then invited to the homes of various congregation members for Sunday dinner, which was a great experience.

Another memory occurred on the bus ride home that afternoon. It was Sunday, January 15, 1967, the Sunday of the 1st Super Bowl. The game was between the Green Bay Packers and Kansas City Chiefs. Green Bay, led by Coach Vince Lombardi, won the game quite easily. It made the long trip home go faster.

Record 10–1
Roberts Rally Holds off Evangel 5

As the season progressed, we became used to winning. We were surprised and a little dumbfounded when Evangel College of Springfield, Missouri, visited us. They nearly upset us. Playing at home, we trailed most of the game. Evangel, a Christian liberal arts college with an enrollment of 815, was very similar to Roberts. Evangel was one of the few teams I ever saw who could handle our half-court zone press. Their passing was so effective that we were just running around and trying to catch up on defense, not even able to get a double team and not coming close to stealing the ball. It almost seemed like they were toying with us. But the press got us out of our funk, and toward the end of the game, we went on a 32 to 13 run to emerge with the 78–72 win.

Record 11–1
Roberts Gains 58–52 Victory over Alfred University

Although a week earlier, Alfred beat a good University of Rochester team, they were no powerhouse. We expected to whip them without much resistance. Were we ever wrong? The Saxons played a slow-down game, hoping to frustrate our fast-paced offense. They did, and we trailed at half-time. Coach Hughes was so frustrated with our big men at halftime that he called them a bunch of "lumbering oaks." We didn't laugh when he said that, but over the years, it remained in our memories and institutional and team consciousness. We have had many laughs over the years regarding "lumbering oaks." We again turned it on during the second half and won by 6. Alfred's slowdown was before there was a thirty-second clock. It really messed up our offensive numbers.

Record 12–1
First Annual Monroe County College
Basketball Tournament

This tournament was a big deal. It became, and we did not know it at the time, one of the longest-running in-season small college tournaments in the country, stretching out over fifty years. It was a great event, and it really put the spotlight on local small college basketball.

The first tournament pitted Brockport State, St. John Fisher, RIT (Rochester Institute of Technology,) and Roberts Wesleyan against each other. Over the years, other colleges such as Hobart, University of Rochester, and Alfred were added.

First Round, Roberts against Brockport

We crushed Brockport by a score of 92–66. The next day's headline in the *Democrat and Chronicle* read, "Roberts Wins 13th in a Row." The article went on to say that Roberts outclassed Brockport in all departments. Bill Bachmann and Glen Schultz led the winners with 27 and 20 points, respectively. Bachmann led both teams with 20 rebounds, and Paul Crowell came off the bench to score 14 points and grab 11 rebounds. The attendance was near one thousand.

Roberts Defeats RIT to Win Championship

In the finals, we took on RIT and defeated them 92–81 to win the championship. Bill Bachmann was awesome. He pulled down 25 rebounds, scored 28 points, and won the most valuable player award. Frank Carter was named to the all-tournament team. Dale Easterly stepped up to play a major defensive role as he took on RIT's big scorer, Jim Robinson. The *Democrat and Chronicle* reported that Easterly was given a starting nod purely on his ability to stop Robinson. The newspaper reported that he was well-chosen for the role.

A turn away, standing-room-only crowd of 1,400 was on hand.

Record 14–1
Roberts Tops McMaster University

The Associated Press reported that Roberts Wesleyan streaked to its fifteenth consecutive victory behind the sharp shooting of Bill Bachmann with a 100-82 drubbing of McMasters University of Hamilton, Ontario. Bachmann was a high man in this contest with

31 points. The victors' only loss was the first game of this season. At one point in the second half, Roberts led by 35.

Back in the 1960s, Canadian intercollegiate basketball was inferior when compared to teams stateside. Having a Canadian team on your schedule could be checked off in advance as an automatic win. That gap has long since closed.

Record 15–1
Robert Scampers to 16th Straight Win
in Classic Game Buffalo State

Note: This game was so special the author decided to devote several pages to it.

Probably the most significant game in the seventy-five-year history of intercollegiate basketball at Roberts Wesleyan College was played at Churchville-Chilie High School on February 4, 1967. The opponent was Buffalo State, one of the best small college teams in the Northeast. Buff State came to town as a team that Roberts had never beaten. Roberts was winless against State in nine tries.

Both teams brought some impressive performance numbers to the contest. Buff State was an excellent defensive team, giving up an average of only 67 points per game. Roberts was averaging 94 points per game. Other statistical distinctions included:

- Buff State was ranked number 1 in the State University of New York Conference.
- Roberts came into the game having won fifteen games in a row.
- The Raiders had won forty-three of their last fifty regular season games.

This was probably the best team ever to walk on the floor for Buff State, and the same was true for Roberts.

For this particular game, there was a different atmosphere present, almost rock concert-like. The Roberts' fans, always a vibrant and passionate throng, were even more vibrant than usual, and they were

LOUD. Dave Warner, the *Democrat and Chronicle* sports reporter who covered the game, stated, "The partisan crowd made enough noise to take care of a combined armistice and New Year's Eve celebration."[3] Everyone in the house knew it was a huge game, and what made it even more mesmerizing was that the outcome was very much in doubt. Each team was capable of winning. By the way, Buff State recently sharpened its skills against Division I, Niagara University, and powerful Gannon College. The Orangemen were not afraid to take on the elites.

There were individual stars as well. Frank Carter came into the game as the leading scorer for Roberts, averaging 26.1 points per game, and Bill Bachmann was the leading rebounder, with 13.3 per game. For Buffalo, Charlie Davis (who played his high school ball at East High in Rochester) and Al Kozen paced a deep Buff State team that had twelve players who were solid, many of whom would be starting for another team.

The game itself was a very compelling contest and very well played, featuring several lead changes, some spectacular dunks, and tremendous demonstrations of athletic ability and intensity. What made this contest so memorable, however, was the environment in which the game was played. In terms of seating capacity, the Churchville-Chili High School gym was somewhat small. Because there had been such a buildup to the game, and because each team brought such outstanding—Roberts (15–1) and Buff State (10–3), this game was seen as "the clash of the titans," and everyone wanted to be there. The gym could only seat 1,000, and there were probably 1,500 people who showed up, requiring the fire marshals to turn away about 500 people. During these two years (1965–67), Roberts' games were always a "hot" ticket, and the stands were always full. However, the stands usually did not fill up until the end of the Jayvee game. (Note: Fans would also get to the games early to see our warm-ups and warm-up drills, which were quite entertaining— especially the dunking drill.) On this night, the stands were full before the

---

[3] Taken from the sports section of the *Democrat & Chronicle*, February 5, 1967 edition.

Jayvee game started. People not only wanted to get a good seat; they wanted to make sure they got a seat. Fans were forced to stand on the sidelines to watch the game. Some fans managed to climb to an open area above the entrance to the gym. They were literally "hanging from the rafters."

As you can see, this was not an average, run-of-the-mill game. This was a game for the ages, a game that may come along once every fifty years or so.

When the teams entered the gym to warm up, Buffalo was welcomed with a chorus of boos. Roberts then took the floor to a thunderous ovation—one of the loudest I ever heard. When warm-ups were over, the invocation was given, the National Anthem was played, and the starters were introduced. Then the game got under-way. Roberts started sluggishly, and suddenly, we were down 13–4. At that point, Buffalo's brilliant starting guard, Benjamin Blumen, got a steal and headed in for a wide-open layup. To the surprise of everyone in the building, he missed it, and Roberts came roaring back. That miss provided the change in momentum that we needed. We quickly got the score close, but it was not until 4:20 left in the half that we, too, had our first lead.

The *Democrat and Chronicle* article the next day stated, "Keith Morre, one of several Raider heroes, gave Roberts a big lift with its first lead as he swished a jumper. Noel Smith came off the bench to hit Glen Schultz with a pretty give-and-go, and Roberts was on fire." The article went on to say that State regained a one-point lead at the onset of the second half, but Frank Carter made a three-point play, and Roberts never trailed again.

The final score was 91–81, Roberts, although at one point we were up by 16. Roberts was led in scoring by Frank Carter with 28, Bill Bachmann with 22, and Keith Morre with 21. How appropriate it was that our three seniors had perhaps their greatest combined scoring effort (71 points) in this game.

Coach Hughes was masterful as he led us through the contest. He never panicked when we got down. He pushed the right buttons and made the right substitutions at the right time. It was his leadership that enabled us to win fifteen games in a row and subsequently set us up for such a dramatic and historic game.

As the clock ran down to the final buzzer, the crowd could not hold back any longer and began a thunderous chant—WE BEAT BUFFALO! WE BEAT BUFFALO! It was cathartic. We believed that Roberts was always perceived as this small church-related school out in the boonies. At the same time, this game did not really prove that we could play with the big boys (we had already proven that), but it did put a little more pride in our chests and bounce in our steps (players and fans) for weeks to come.

On a personal note, I was very proud to have played in this game. I knew it was an historic game. While I only scored one point, I was thrilled to be on the scoreboard. I also provided the starting guards with some valuable rest. In both halves, I brought the ball up the court, set up and ran our Carson-Newman shuffle offense, handled the ball, and got the ball to my teammates. I remember the coach saying, "Dave, go in for Dale." I ripped off my jacket, flew to the scorer's table, and they whistled me in. Immediately, I was in touch with how fast the pace of this game was and how good Buff State really was. As I got us into the Carson-Newman shuffle offense, I had to work much harder to get the ball into the forwards. I felt like I was on the track at the Daytona 500. I knew that I would have to do everything a little quicker than usual. One could tell that Buffalo State was an elite team.

Ah yes, WE BEAT BUFFALO.

*Much of the information on this page comes from a *Democrat and Chronicle* article written by Dave Warner of the *Democrat and Chronicle* Sports staff. The article appeared the morning after the game**

**The statistics were pulled from the game program insert, which was written by Roberts Sports Information Director Harry Hutt,

***Democrat and Chronicle* sports section February 5, 1967

Record 16–1
Roberts' String Snapped by Edinboro State

All good things must come to an end, and our winning streak did just that. For the winning streak to come to an end would require an opponent who was big, physical, and talented. This opponent would have a better chance if they caught us on their home court. Edinboro met all the criteria, and after sixteen straight wins, we came up short, and we bowed to Edinboro, 89–78 in Pennsylvania.

Edinboro had two stars, Daryl Meachum and Lynn Nelson, who were both six foot seven, taller than anyone on our team. Meachum was drafted by the Cincinnati Royals of the NBA in the 1967 draft. He was the only player I ever saw drive the center of the lane and dunk on us.

We fell behind by 17 points in the second half. Then we pulled to within 7 with four and a half minutes to go. However, that was as close as we got. Bill Bachman was our leading scorer with 35 points. It was a long bus ride home, literally and figuratively.

Record 16–2
Bad Time in Beantown

We will never know what happened on this trip. Losing to Edinboro was not pleasant, but it was acceptable. They were a great team. But losing to Eastern Nazarene was unfathomable. They were a mediocre team—the final score was Eastern Nazarene, 67, and Roberts, 64. I have no words to explain what happened. We were just so flat. Everyone expected us to win by 20 points or more.

Record 16–3

The next night, we took on Gordon College in Wenham, Massachusetts. We were shaky in the beginning, trailing 20–12 before we went on a 10–0 run that propelled us to a 49–37 lead at the half. In the second half, we cruised to a 100–75 victory. Bill Bachmann led the way with 23 points, followed by Frank Carter with 22 points, and Keith Moore with 21. Glen Schultz had 16. Good things happened when our three seniors broke the 20-point mark.

Record 17–3
Roberts Defeats RIT

It was that time in the season when we were going down the homestretch. After the next four to five games, the careers of Frank Carter, Bill Bachmann, and Keith Moore would be over. We were starting to focus on the NAIA tournament, but we still had three tough games to play, including RIT, Alliance College, and St. John Fisher. Despite our outstanding record, a tournament bid was not automatic. I can't remember the details, but I am sure Coach Hughes emphasized that we would have to win all three games to be assured of a bid.

RIT succumbed to us by a score of 79–73 in the Ritter-Clark gym on the campus of RIT. According to the *Democrat and Chronicle*, a crowd of 1,500 was on hand. The win was not easy for the Raiders. *Democrat and Chronicle* columnist Dave Warner said that "after taking a 12-point lead, they became as careless as a sailor on payday."

Record 18–3
NAIA District 19 Playoffs
Game One

This game is what we played for all year. We took on Millersville State in a best two-out-of-three series. The first game was played on a neutral court at St. John Fisher. The winner of this series would go to Kansas City for the national tournament. Going into this game, Millersville ranked eighth in scoring in the nation. Millersville entered the tournament with a record of 19–5. They were averaging 104 points per game. Roberts played a catch-up game for seven minutes with thirty-three seconds remaining in the first half until 8:40 left in the second half when Frank Carter hit from the corner, tying the score at 71. Before the Raiders made a comeback, they trailed by as many as 13 points in the first half. With forty-five seconds remaining in regulation play and the score tied at 88 all, Millersville controlled a jump ball. They then played for the last shot but missed with two seconds remaining, sending the game into overtime. To make a long story short, we lost in overtime 99 to 96.

Record 0–1
Game Two

After losing the first game, we needed to win two straight games to make it to the national tournament in Kansas City. Plus, we had to go on the road to Millersville, Pennsylvania. The game was on a Monday night. We had planned to drive down and play ON THE SAME DAY. However, we were faced with a huge problem—a big snowstorm was settling in that day. We decided to fly. We were able to secure tickets for Coach Hughes and seven players. Everyone else would have to fly on standby. In those days, it was easy to secure standby tickets. We all thought we would get on the flight. We did not. All passengers showed up, and some of us got bumped onto a later flight.

To make a long story short, in a few hours, we were at Philadelphia Airport waiting in line to get a rent-a-car. It took forever. The clock was ticking. The game was at 8:00 p.m., and we were in Philadelphia, half an hour away. It began to dawn on us that we were not going to make it. arry Hutt

Harry Hutt was speeding down the expressway. One of us turned on the radio, and we found the game that we were now late for. We were listening to our team playing without us. When we arrived, I had never moved so fast. The second half had just started. I got into my uniform as quickly as I could and rushed up to the gym. Coach put me right in. I had no chance to warm up.

We lost 77–74 in overtime. Carter, Bachmann, and Moore had played in their last game. We all felt terrible to end that way. An era had come to an end.

CHAPTER 15

The Greatest Homecoming Ever

It was a long bus ride home—the night before, we lost to Millersville State in Millersville, Pennsylvania. The loss cost us a chance to go to Kansas City and compete in the NAIA National Championship Tournament. This tournament brought together the best thirty-two teams in the nation. The game was an overtime thriller. As we rode home on the bus, we were quite exhausted and disappointed. There was a feeling that we had let our fans down.

A bunch of us were engaged in a game of "Ghost" to pass the time, including Paul Mroz, Barb Rose (the cheerleaders came to the game), and Harry Hutt. A lot of guys slept. We did not have a clue as to what was in store for us in a couple of hours. As the bus chugged into North Chili and headed up Union Street, we started to grab our gear. The bus turned right onto Buffalo Road. We were one-fourth of a mile from home. As I looked ahead on Buffalo Road, the first thing I noticed was several police cars with their lights flashing. My first thought was that there must have been a horrific accident. But it was no accident.

As we rode closer, I could see throngs of people wildly waving their arms and cheering. As the bus pulled up, the crowd surrounded us. The crowd included students, faculty, members of the administration, and members of the community. The entire College community canceled classes and came out to welcome us home. It was a hero's welcome.

As we emerged from the bus, the male students made a bee-line to Frank Carter, Bill Bachmann, and Keith Moore, the three seniors who had just played in their final game. All three of those players were hoisted on the shoulders of the students and carried to Carpenter Hall, where a pep rally was awaiting us. The rest of us walked up Orchard Street, where there were hundreds of people cheering us along the way as we walked to Carpenter Hall.

I could not believe it. It was one of those rare and precious moments that one never forgets. We had a lot of love showered upon us that day.

When we went to Carpenter Hall, the players were separated from the crowd and ushered to the back stairway, which led to the dining hall. A door separated us from the crowd. With the students now assembled in the dining hall, the program began. Each player was introduced by Student Body President Art Brown, who served as MC. He did a masterful job.

I was the third or fourth player introduced. Art's words were (and I will never forget them), "And how about that little point guard who never played high school ball, Dave Scribner." As I walked across the floor, the applause rained down on me, and I was never prouder. I had come a long way from being told by a doctor when I was in ninth grade that I would not be allowed to play basketball because of a heart murmur. Now I was a well-known athlete on the greatest team in Roberts' history.

There were several speeches. Then song sheets were passed out, and the entire throng sang a song. The name of the song was "Welcome Back Raiders," and it was sung to the tune of "Hello Dolly."

This experience brought home to me how much Roberts was like one big family. I was proud to be a part of it. This homecoming was one of three watershed events that I experienced during the 1966-67 season. The other two were our smashing win over Buffalo State and winning the first-ever Monroe County Championship.

Fifty-Five Years Later

This section is a reflection of the player's lives and thoughts on the team and coach. In 2022, fifty-five years after they finished their playing careers, the Raider Gazette posed the following questions to each of them:

- How did being a member of this team affect your life?
  - o Your outlook on life?
  - o Did it have any effect on your career? If so, how?
  - o And did it affect your self-confidence?
- Pick the experience or event that had the greatest impact on you or was the most meaningful to you. Describe the experience in as much detail as possible and describe your reaction.

As you read the responses, please remember that the questions may have been answered in an order that is different from the order that you see above.

Their answers, contained in the pages below, were poignant and compelling.

Back row: Harry Hutt (assistant coach), Darwin Chapman, Keith Moore, Dale Easterly, Glenn Schultz, Paul Crowell, Herm Schwingle, Noel Smith, Ralph Roach, Paul Mroz (manager) *Sitting row*: Stan Ziblut, Dave Scribner, Coach Hughes, Bill Bachmann, Frank Carter

CHAPTER 16

Reflections by Coach Bill Hughes

The first person we will hear from is Coach Bill Hughes. The coach will talk about the importance of discipline, setting goals, and character.

To all the members of the "greatest basketball team" in RWC history:

We have all been asked to answer the very important question, "How has your life been affected by your experiences as a part of the basketball teams at Roberts Wesleyan College, and what did you take away that specifically affected your life, career, confidence, etc.? So much meaningful happened to all of us that it is impossible to really do justice in four hundred words, but I will comment on several aspects I experienced.

I came to RWC in the fall of 1961. I had three years of actually living the role Gene Hackman played in *Hoosiers* as I cut my teeth as head coach in two different Illinois high schools in one of the most extremely fanatical basketball areas in the entire state.

My beginning was not a smashing success. I lasted six weeks as coach at Oakwood High School before they fired me because I pushed the little darlings too hard. Can you believe that? I managed to hold my next job for two years before President Voller asked me to fly out and interview for his coaching position. I did the interview and he offered me the head coaching basketball job and AD responsibilities. Why, to this day, I will never understand. He must have seen something in this twenty-six-year-old kid. He made it very clear he wanted a disciplined, winning program, with emphasis on the discipline part.

Through my experiences as a player and having played for five different coaches, plus the lessons learned in my three years of coaching, I did have my mind made up concerning what it takes to really be a winner. I felt then, and still do to this day, that among those requirements are discipline, goals, and character. When I left RWC six years later, I took away an even greater understanding of the importance of all three in succeeding in not just basketball, but life itself. I hoped I could instill all three in all of you, my players.

- *Discipline*

One of the main reasons we were so successful those last two years was we were a very disciplined team, something we had learned over our first two struggling years. Being a game of mistakes, we made fewer than our opponents. We knew how to win with the right style of play for us, which was our wide-open run/press play. I had always pushed everyone as hard as I could, from the stars to the last man on the bench. Our up-tempo style required a very strong bench. Our bench beat everyone else's bench every time.

Considering Glen, Stan, and Ken starters, without Noel, Dale, Herman, Dave, Paul, and Ralph, we NEVER could have accomplished what we did. All our team and individual accomplishments would not have happened without our "tremendous bench." My life and coaching takeaway learned at RWC was never to underestimate the value of developing a great bench. In short, we beat thirty-eight out of forty-four teams because we worked harder, played smarter, and always played as a team—THAT TOOK DISCIPLINE!

- *Goals*

Another takeaway that I learned as being very important in both basketball and life is that you must have goals. Establishing goals was one of the best coaching moves I made at RWC. I am sure without them, we never would have achieved what we did. You all will recall that around the beginning of our 1965–66 season, I began to tell you all about the greatest basketball tournament in our country, THE NATIONAL NAIA BASKETBALL TOURNAMENT.

Gentlemen, at that time, in the early '60s, before most of the colleges recruited black players, the caliber of the thirty-two teams that made it to the Kansas City finals could have beaten 50 to 75 percent of the NCAA Division I teams. The phrase "Dare To Dream Big" comes to mind. I must have been a little crazy to challenge the team at Little Roberts Wesleyan to even think about making it to those finals and joining those tremendous, high-level, and powerful programs.

We had not done anything yet to even realistically think about such a thing. But I sold the idea to all of you, and you know the rest of the story. Despite all the things that were against us, like no gym, no real budget, no rich basketball tradition, and no encouraging fat cat alumni, we made a "heck" of a run at it, and but for a few points here and there, would have found our team in Kansas City with the rest of the great teams. Ours was a truly unbelievable accomplishment. But then our whole story was so amazing, partly because we did dare to "dream big."

- *Character*

Another wonderful takeaway I believed in even more and always used in my continued coaching was character. I never realized just how important the character of my players was until I left RWC and was in different atmospheres.

Most of you were so fortunate to have grown up in Christian homes and circles. Because of that, all of you were able to accept being pushed to the max, putting the team's interest above your own, and having great love and respect for each other. I am sure that without that type of personal character and internal spirit, we would never have accomplished what we did. After leaving RWC, I always tried to recruit players of high character, and I found many fine men but never a full team as I enjoyed at RWC. I took away a greater understanding of the amazing value of character after leaving all of you.

I have told you all this before. I really did not realize fully what we really did as a basketball team. When I look at the accomplishments we achieved as a team, such as being ranked among the top 40 teams out of over 650 colleges and universities, being among the top highest-scoring teams with over 90 PPG, and being among the top 25 teams with the highest winning margin – beating our opponents by around 30 points every game, I am amazed. Individually, our teams produced an NAIA All-American Honorable Mention, who also was among the top 25 leading scorers among over 7,000 players in the NAIA with a 25 PPG average. We also produced a rebounder that was ranked 11th to rebounder with around 17 rpg— again among the same group of 7,000 other players. We also won many fine tournament championships, placing many of our players on the all-tournament teams and MVP selections.

How DID WE DO ALL THIS? I don't rightly know, but I sure am glad that God let me be part of it. What about you? "Coach?"

What Would I Tell a Young RWC Student about Our Team?

I would want him to understand that this team of 1966–67 and 1967–68 was a "special team" and why. Here are a few of those reasons that he or she would probably understand.

- If you are special, you do things that others are unable to do. This collection of special players broke, then set almost every single basketball record that still exists today.
- The members of a special team must be special individuals as well. The team's leading scorer, Frank Carter, was among the top 25 leading scorers in the nation, which consisted of over 650 college and university teams made up of over 6,500 players.

Frank averaged over 25 PPG for two years. He was also an All-American Honorable Mention selection, joining only 40 other players among that pool of 6,500 other players. Frank was the best basketball player ever to play at RWC and probably always will be.

The leading rebounder, Bill Bachmann, with over seventeen rebounds per game, was ranked among the top twenty-five rebounders in the entire NAIA. This is what it means to be a special players. Every other member of that special team also contributed in their own special way.

- This special basketball team was coached by a special young coach, Bill Hughes, who in later years would amass many individual honors and awards such as two Athletic Hall of Fame inductions, Coach of the Year awards, conference championships, NCAA Division One Coaching, etc.
- Strange as it may seem, this special little program has as its "major goal" to reach NAIA NATIONAL FINAL PLAYOFFS. Only the top 32 District Champions out of the 650 NAIA teams earned the right to compete in Kansas City for the national title. This special team missed two years in a row in the district finals by just a few points. This success was accomplished without a gym, a very low operating budget, no athletic scholarships, and no "fat cat" alumni or successful tradition to build on.
- Perhaps the greatest reason that made this group of young men so special was what their influence did for the school. Because of the tremendous success on the court and the personal lives lived around the entire campus every day, there developed a wonderful PRIDE that was shared by faculty, staff, administrators, and the entire student body. Everyone wanted to be, by extension, a part of the team.
- Campus spirit was never higher, and attending the Saturday night games meant a packed gym and getting there a couple of hours early to get in.
- This special team was so admired by so many that after many years, the decision was made to elect the entire team

into the RWC Athletic Hall of Fame. Never had this kind of honor been given to any team in any sport!

The campus was changed so much for the good by this special team, and you just had to be there to understand it!

Years 1985–2023

In 1985, I began a "new life" by moving back to my Texas home, where I have remained for the last thirty-eight years. After experiencing a family breakup, the move to Dallas (Plano) was the beginning of a "new start." With coaching out of the picture, I began my new career in real estate. I have developed many skills, ideas, and plans over the years that will serve me well in the real estate field. I started that career with no money and no contacts, and little by little, I began to see real progress. Over these years in the residential real estate business, I have bought and sold homes, bought and leased homes, and bought, remodeled, and sold condos, single-family homes, and small apartment complexes.

This part is a little unusual. I knew no one down here except for a very few family members. The very first week after arriving from Fredonia, my wonderful mother suggested that I try attending a "parents without partners" weekly social event. I took her suggestion, and that night, I met this pretty, intelligent, and wonderful young lady who would become the love of my life for all these years. Veronica had a ten-year-old son that I have had the privilege of sharing all these years. I have enjoyed being an investor in this great residential market. God has blessed me financially, and now we enjoy our retirement. We spend our time with our dogs, traveling, and summers back in Fredonia. I have played tennis avidly for years. I, with three other friends, organized a senior men's tennis league with over one hundred members. I also organize occasional dinner parties, as well as Christmas and Saint Valentine's Day parties.

We have good friends, and for an old guy, God has blessed me with really good health, except for my walking problems. IT'S ALL GOOD!

CHAPTER 17

What Stan Ziblut Has to Say about Relationships, Friendships, and the Values Coach Instilled

The effect on my life, having been a member of the '65–'66 basketball team, had little to do with wins and losses and everything to do with the friendships developed during my time with RWC basketball. The effect of the success we shared loses some of its luster over time, but the friendships developed become much more important and satisfying.

The moments I now treasure most were the times and the times spent off the court: The times I spent with Bill when I visited him in Florida and the times he visited me in Wisconsin, and the times I spent with Frank over breakfast when I visited my mother in the falls. The ability of both Bill and Frank to entertain with their storytelling always impressed me. The only difference in their stories was that Frank had the ability to make them sound almost believable!

The one year I played alongside Keith turned into a lifelong friendship that I treasure and enjoy. The friendship I developed with Dave and Paul, who were freshmen when I was a senior, happened after my playing days were done. Our golf success at Roberts golf outings did not match our success on the court, which just proves friendships survive even with dismal team performance. I have

Herm, Glen, and Noel to count as friends. All of these individuals have become lifelong friends because of RWC basketball.

Certainly, Coach Hughes had a huge role to play in all of the abovementioned. It says a great deal about a man who one can call a great coach and a great friend—more on this in my second response.

The event that had the greatest impact on my life actually happened in the '63–'64 and '64–'65 timeframe—those two years left an impression on me that influenced my life and career. That impression was one of the absolute necessity of having individuals working as a team versus a team of individuals.

The '63–'64 team had some very talented players who referred to themselves as Gun 1, Gun 2, and Jr. Gun. As you can assume, team camaraderie was not the best, and our record reflects that. We had individual stars but not "team" stars.

Those three were gone by the '64–'65 season, two by choice and one by tragedy. I have often wondered what Gun 1, Gun 2, and Jr. Gun thought when they realized that "Top Gun" had arrived from Niagara Falls. They would have had to be a little embarrassed because Frank would never have referred to himself as "Top Gun." Frank was never into self-promotion. I knew of Frank's ability and his character, having played against him in high school.

I believe Coach decided he would not tolerate a team made of individuals but wanted individuals to make up a team. With Frank, Bill, and Coach allowing Keith to return, Coach knew he had three individuals (whom I think were the three irreplaceable members of our team) to form the core of a successful team.

It was Coach's ability to keep egos in check through discipline, when required, yet in a manner not to result in resentment on a player's part. He had certain principles that he held firmly and exercised fairly. His character influenced all of us. As a result, a great coach also became a great friend.

That concept of having individuals leading by example rather than by dictate has stayed with me in my professional and personal life. In my business, I was careful to associate myself with those who shared that vision of teamwork, not one of Gun 1, 2, or 3.

CHAPTER 18

Dave Scribner Shares How He Made the Team

I believe that we were fortunate (and we probably did not realize it at the time) to be forged in the competitive fires ignited and stoked by Coach Hughes as he attempted to get us to perform not just at a high level but at the highest level of which we were capable. We ran a gauntlet every day (can you say practice?) that toughened us and melded us together as a true team. I do not recall any selfishness on this team. I just remember how we battled in practice and ran those suicide drills for a coach, always striving to do our best.

A word about coach, when he spoke, I listened. He taught me many things. Two of the most important included:

- *Preparation.* I always thought that our opponents were thoroughly scouted and that we had a game plan designed to help us win.
- *Thinking big.* He judged us on a national scope and challenged us to share his vision.

So if a player experienced this combination of preparations, practice diligence, application, and follow-through and then looked at the performance output of this team and the respect that the team engendered on campus, that player would have to feel a rush from this throughout life—a rush that will never wane. *Whenever I was asked in my professional life to perform or deliver something on the job that required a Herculean effort, I knew that, in a way, I had already done it.*

After making up the questions (with a lot of help from Coach Huges), I am struggling to find the most honest answers that live in my heart. When I arrived on campus in the fall of '65, no one knew who I was. I was not recognized as a "hot" freshman recruit, and I knew nothing about Roberts Wesleyan basketball.

I had a tremendous chip on my shoulder as I had buried a lot of "old" anger deep in my gut. This anger was generated when I was a high school freshman. Despite being one of the best players in my school, I was told that I could not play basketball because of a heart murmur (which I gradually outgrew). I was stunned, devastated, and outraged. But, somehow, I managed to pick myself up, dust myself off, and put my nose to the grindstone. I got a job at the Batavia YMCA (where I played a lot of basketball) and concentrated on my studies for the next three years.

I decided to enroll at Roberts Wesleyan for several reasons, none of which had anything to do with basketball. After arriving on campus, I started joining pickup games at the "pit" and began to develop a basketball identity among my fellow students. I won't bore you with the details, but the rest is history. I just missed making the varsity as a freshman, but I gained valuable experience playing on the Freshman Team. Paul Crowell and I were the leading freshman scorers. Paul and I developed a tremendous bond over the years. He was one of the most rugged and raw-boned players I ever played with. When I was able to get the ball to him under the basket, one of three things always happened: (1) he would score, (2) he would get fouled, or (3) he would put his opponent through the wall. Paul is one of the finest individuals I ever met, and I love him like a brother. I feel that way about all my teammates.

The experience that had the greatest impact on me was making the varsity team as a sophomore and the training process I put myself through to achieve this. Making the team was a gateway for me to have some of the greatest experiences of my life. It also gave me the opportunity to play on the greatest team, with the greatest team-mates, in front of the greatest fans, and for the greatest coach that anyone could ask for. But I had to make the team. Making that team was no cakewalk. The team was loaded with talented players. There were only two openings. Jr. College players were being recruited.

The perseverance I developed in high school surfaced in me, and I worked my tail off during the summer between my freshman and sophomore years. I would work for hours on my ball-handling alone. It paid of big time. I made the team. I played my way into the rotation; I played significant minutes and contributed to the team's success. So, in a way, the competitive culture created by Coach Hughes, as well as the high standards of excellence he set, served me by giving me something to strive for and work towards. All players, whether they admit it or not, want to play for a coach who demands excellence. Coach Huges demanded it, and he got it. In the process, with the grace of God, I became a decent college player and, hopefully, a better teammate.

Oh yes, and about that anger, anger always comes out eventually. My anger came out on the court, and I channeled it against the opponents we played. I wasn't all that great a player, but I don't think that any opponent liked it when I guarded him. I would put him through misery.

I will be eternally grateful to God, Roberts Wesleyan College, and Coach Bill Hughes for giving me the opportunity of a lifetime. Coach, thanks for being a man of principle who always held up high standards. Those standards have served me well throughout my life.

Looking back on the last thirty to fifty years, I would have to say that I have been blessed to have had a very good life. Fortunately for me, many people have contributed to my life, including the members of my team. I know this goes back more than fifty years, but I would like to thank all of you for being such great teammates.

As far as what I would like today's students to know—that is a tough question. I guess I would like the student to know of the character, leadership, and teamwork that made us a team that rarely comes along. This team also had strong talent and a no-nonsense coach who absolutely demanded and received our best efforts. But this team was more than just a good team that won a lot of games and set a lot of records.

As I said in a speech I made at Coach Hughes' Hall of Fame induction, it seemed that this team left an indelible mark on the college. This team was:

- Transcendent
- Transformational
- Triumphant

By transcendent, I mean great, better, more notable than anything that came before. Our team transcended all others. I know that sounds like bragging. Sorry.

By transformational, I mean that this team produced big changes in how basketball was treated at Roberts. Huge crowds started coming to the games. The Rochester press featured us more than ever before. A strong school spirit was present on campus, and part of that could be attributed to the team.

Triumphant means more than winning. It means winning big games. Buff State was an example. It also means winning certain games in a big way. Scores like 102–58 were not uncommon. Our average winning margin was 15 points per game, one of the best in the nation.

I would want this student to know that this team was special.

CHAPTER 19

Paul Crowell and the Impact of the Team on His Life

Being a member of the "team" has had a definite impact on my life. At the time, it seemed like a lot of hard practices and long bus/car trips (Winona Lake, Plattsburg, Potsdam, Boston, Pikeville, Troy State), but those built a sense of purpose and drive to be your best. I came to campus as a "little lost farm boy" and left as an adult. Much of that growth was a result of being a part of the team. Even the "gentle and kindly" education from Bach about not wearing white socks with dress clothes. He did have a way! We developed a common bond and focus because of all our shared efforts. It is great to know that we all are still friends and have these memories of effort and success. I know that my adult career had this "background music" to always remind me that effort and discipline would lead to positive results. For this, I am always grateful for being a part of us.

For the history students of today, we had a lot of fun back in the day but worked really hard to be better than the day before. You need to understand some of the limitations we thought of as normal—one serving of food per meal, no open buffet lines (I need to go back to that). There was no training room other than a set of barbells on a couple of barrels in the Carp basement. Despite it all, we grew stronger and better. Research the Varsity R tournaments in the spring.

Those were some great games, and many nonvarsity players were involved. I think that is something we were lucky to have—a real sense of community and belonging. It wasn't you or me; it was us.

CHAPTER 20

Keith Moore Offers a Deep and Intuitive Understanding of the Team and the Culture That Fostered Its Success

Fortunately, I was not often in the circumstances in my forty-six-year college public relations career as stressful as our two twenty-minute Buffalo State halves or as low percentage as one of my foul shots. I'm grateful to Frank for bringing others along on his amazing sports ride. He was such an amazing athlete and friend. Bachmann was a great source of humor but also an amazingly resourceful offensive force. Coach, of course, insisted on us being in wonderful condition and giving our best in every game. Harry, too, will perpetually have a soft spot in my heart. I was confident before the games because I knew our second team was better than most opponents. We were winning and that built confidence in me that I possibly had little right to take for granted. But I still do today.

I have a collective mental hug surrounding all memories of those years. My primary recollections are of each of the coaches and players who contributed to the thirteen straight wins in 1966 and sixteen straight wins in 1967. Our discipline, focus, and team habits taught me to persist at points where others would give up. I usually made a point of working longer hours and completing call after call even though other workers had stopped caring. And this next observation applied to our teams, yes, but also to our classmates. If a graduate from Roberts promised to do a job, we did it. No excuses. No missed deadlines. I have been shocked at how true that has been wherever I've worked.

Roberts' 1960s basketball fortunes were historic and unexpected—no famous recruits enrolled. Frank Carter, for example, was a not-recruited high school basketball player since he had broken a leg and missed his final high school season. He came to Roberts without fanfare and stayed for four years. He wound up as one of the tops in the school's history in scoring. Bill Bachmann came from a huge high school near Pittsburgh but was not highly recruited either (to my knowledge). His bunny-hop jumping was like none other anywhere. He also stayed for four years. He wound up as the best rebounder in school history and was an excellent scorer. Both ranked among statistical leaders in small colleges nationally.

Somehow, basketball spirit permeated the campus during those years. It was cultivated in tiny Carpenter Hall gym's ad hoc tournaments held on weekends and when the sport was not in season. Pickup games there developed skills that expanded the talents of varsity players, campus intramural athletes, bystanders, and faculty participants. Challenging games raised the competitive instincts of everyone who performed in them and ultimately carried over to varsity competitions against other intercollegiate teams.

Roberts has no locker facilities or training room. It had no trainer. It played all its practices and games in a nearby high school with one thousand seats. When the high school gym was unavailable, practices and scrimmages were staged on Carp Hall's undersized concrete floor (about seventy-five feet by forty feet with no sideline space for team benches). An overhanging balcony held those students at mealtimes, waiting their turns in line for entry into the cafeteria.

And while Roberts had clean, attractive uniforms, it traveled by vans and a vintage bus that ran only most of the time. When Roberts went to the NAIA regionals via air, the school's budget didn't permit the entire team to fly at full fare, so half of the team flew standby and missed the first half of the final game.

Athletes Stan Ziblut, Herm Schwingle, Keith Moore, Glenn Schultz, Paul Crowell, Noel Smith, Dave Scribner, Dale Easterly and

Ralph Roach put indelible stamps on the court as starters for 2-4 years. Fortunately, no serious injuries sidelined any of them. None of them received basketball scholarships, and they attended Roberts for other reasons: for academic specialties and for faith-based or career-oriented goals.

The architect who designed their success, Coach Bill Hughes, was an Illinois high school coach who was only slightly than the Roberts players he inherited. His dedication to basketball was paramount, but his workload also included coaching soccer and conducting athletic director duties. Collectively, the group hated losing. No one more than Coach Hughes. They hated losing so much that they began to establish winning streaks of eight, thirteen, and sixteen games in a row. Relying on an intimidating half-court press with man-to-man pressure at other times, winning, they found, was more fun than losing. The team began to build faith in their individual and orchestrated abilities. As they gained comfort with each other, they frequently blew out opponents, and their confidence and reputation grew.

Hughes and Assistant Coach Harry Hutt pulled Roberts basketball out of its previous concentration on simply putting a team together to play basketball against other teams. They pushed Roberts beyond that focus on operations and contests to a focus on developing Roberts' standing as a basketball power among colleges nationwide.

Hughes's perseverance against heavy odds and his persistence in managing his diverse workloads often exceeded the expectations of his most driven and obsessive players. He ran conditioning drills that still bring chills to the survivors, and he tolerated no "lollygagging" or "freelancing."

The coaches researched new offenses to install and compared the team's statistical records with others in a broad national context, always keeping in sight the goal of performing in the NAIA national tournament in Kansas City. Roberts, once a college with a basketball team that played other colleges without notice for years, was, under their leadership, now one of the best small college basketball teams within its region and, at times, one of the best nationally.

During two seasons, the team played in the regional NAIA playoffs. These were the first in school history. Coach Hughes was selected by his peers as the NAIA Regional Coach of the Year. One year offensively, Robert's pressing defense/fast-break offense averaged more than 90 points a game. The team did not lose a home game during the junior and senior years of Carter and Bachmann (1965–'67).

Eventually, that Carp Hall gym disappeared. It was turned into other uses. Roberts was able to do that because it built its own gymnasium, Voller Athletic Center, named for President Elwood A. Voller, who presided during the period of its 1960s basketball halcyon days. Several seeds were planted in this period for today's Redhawks and their men's and women's NCAA Division II basketball programs.

CHAPTER 21

Glen Schultz on Values and His Daily Walk with the Lord

I find it difficult to put into words the impact being a part of the RWC basketball team had on my life. As I have thought about these questions, two words come to my mind: *singlemindedness* and *wholeheartedness*.

Both words describe what Coach Hughes always expected out of each one of us. We had to approach every practice with a focus like I had never experienced before in my life. Every detail, from warm-ups to dry running the shuffle offense to running the half-court trap press, had to be done as if the outcome of the next game depended on it.

Of course, this carried over in everything we did while at Roberts. If I recall, our team had a very good GPA in the classroom. Again, I attribute much of that to the discipline and commitment Coach instilled in us every time we laced up our sneakers.

These two character qualities have stayed with me throughout my personal and professional lives. However, the greatest impact my playing experience has had on me has been in my everyday walk with the Lord.

The singlemindedness I had to have as a player has caused me to understand what God expects out of me as one of His children. Paul wrote in Colossians 3:1–2 these words:

> Since, then, you have been raised with Christ, set your hearts on things above, where Christ is seated at the right hand of God. Set your minds on things above, not on earthly things.

As far as what I would like current students at Roberts to know, it is hard to put into words what I experienced as a member of the '65–'67 Hall of Fame team. I guess I would want the students to know that we weren't about trying to be stars. We loved each other and were thrilled to have the privilege to play together. We were not just teammates; we were friends. We enjoyed each other's company and wanted to see each one of us succeed. We were willing to pay whatever price required to become the best we were capable of. We weren't discouraged or distracted by failure but motivated to learn and become better. There is no doubt in my mind that God was doing something special, and I just wanted to be a part of it.

CHAPTER 22

Noel Smith on How He Landed a Great Job at Kodak because of His Basketball Experience at Roberts

After I graduated from RWC, I taught high school for a year. During that time, I kept in touch with Ken Curtis, who had been hired by Kodak and was working in Minnesota as a sales rep. One day during the school year, Curt called me to let me know that Kodak was hiring. Thinking that I would probably enjoy selling more than teaching, I requested an application. After I filled out the application, my wife, Winnie, reviewed it and wondered why I didn't list anything under honors and awards. I added information to include the All-Tournament Team at the 1968 Monroe County College Tournament, which we won. I received an invite for an interview, and to my amazement, two or the three men that interviewed me knew all about the outstanding Roberts Wesleyan College basketball teams over the last three or four years.

While they should have been asking me "Why should we hire you?" or "How do you know that you'd be a successful?", we talked basketball during most of the interview. I was so confident that I'd get the job that I canceled an interview at Xerox later that day. The bottom line is that having had the opportunity to be part of a fabulous college basketball program opened the door for my career job at Kodak.

What Could I Tell a Current RWC Student about the '65–'67 Team?

We were players who came from diverse backgrounds and had both character and competitiveness. We were coached by a young, talented, no-nonsense coach who quickly earned our respect. We were a group of players that liked each other and were totally focused on the goal.

Ralph Roach on Team Family 1966–67

At the beginning of the 1966–67 basketball season, I played for Harry's Hawks freshman team for five games before I was brought up to the varsity. I was awed as I was the only freshman on the team. I wasn't sure what to expect. It didn't take long before I felt accepted. Several veteran players on the team took me in as one of their own. For example, Frank said to me, "No such thing as can't get a shot off" was one of many. We battled each other during practice "to help make each other better." I had proof, as all of us did—bruised shoulders from the Carson Newman shuffle. The players bonded together as a team family and achieved a tremendous amount of success, including the Chase Lincoln Championship. I was proud to be a part of it all.

We traveled together as a family team on long trips, and I had my first plane trip, arriving in Millersville late for the NAIA district finals. I know that the players and coaches who arrived ahead of us were worried about the rest of the team's family. We arrived at half-time.

I'm truly thankful to be a part of this tremendous team family. Since I've moved on from these days, these memories will stay with me. I have been part of a coach's family, a teacher's family, a basketball family, a soccer family, a tennis family, and most importantly, my own family (wife, two sons, and three grandchildren). Family is a big part of my life.

The event that had the greatest impact on me was Bill Bachmann's speech at a banquet in 2017 honoring the *best* two-year basketball team in RWC's history. I believe everyone connected to this team was in attendance. Bill sat when he spoke because he didn't have the energy to stand. (In my words, this is how I remember what Bill said). He said that he wasn't afraid of leaving this earth. In fact, he was ready to meet his Lord and Savior. *Wow.* What a statement. I will never forget his words and will carry them with me forever.

My Thoughts on the RWC Hall of Fame Basketball Team

Like a traditional family, those at its head influence and guide its members. Achievements, accomplishments, and success at this level do not happen without strong and dedicated leadership. For RWC basketball, it was Coach Hughes. He led us through well-structured practices, and he possesses a natural way of making modifications during games when needed. I believe he was tough on us during practices because he wanted us to be all that we could be.

From my experience, being a member of the RWC '65–'67 Hall of Fame Team was one highlight of my college experience. We were *very* successful because of Coach Hughes and because we had several very talented players. We got along well together and worked hard as a *team*. To prepare for battling our opponents and to achieve success, we challenged each other in practice and banded together as a *team family*.

Not only did we have a lot of talent on the team, but also its members showed a lot of character. I remember an away tournament in the South. Some players stopped for a bite to eat, and the restaurant staff refused to seat a team member. Because of the way he was treated, we all walked out of the restaurant.

Some might be tired of my *family* talk; however, I truly believe being a *family* played a significant role in our success.

I would like to thank Coach Hughes and my teammates for being part of a fantastic experience.

CHAPTER 23

Paul Mroz Ph.D. - Team Manager

Being a part of the Raider basketball experience was a learning experience and a motivator, which guided my high school coaching career to come. I not only came in contact with individuals who demonstrated finesse on the court, but I learned by watching a gifted head coach handle and manage the variety of personalities represented in the group. This was particularly valuable to me in my own coaching career as it developed in the years following my Roberts experience.

I will never forget the Buffalo State Game in the Churchville-Chili gym. It truly represented and demonstrated not only the collective ability but also the individual commitment and spirit that marked the greatest era of Roberts' basketball. I was *proud* to sit on the bench as the manager!

Many life lessons were learned at Roberts Wesleyan. Many of these lessons came from the Sermon on the Mount. Others came from the lives of professors and coaches and exposure to the institution's culture—a culture where a redemptive philosophy abounds and is practiced. My hopes and prayers are that each student experiences the campus climate that makes Roberts special for each of them.

My advice to every Roberts student is to set your standards and goals as high as possible. Success in life is determined by your willingness to step out of your comfort zone and to work hard at each task.

Education is important since there is no substitute for competence. Work ethic is important, as achievement comes from both perspiration and inspiration. If you are blessed with average ability, success can and will be achieved when coupled with a strong work ethic. "Ora et Labora," pray and work. Remember, all things are possible through Christ Jesus.

Each of these blessings has made me aware that Jesus is King! As Matthew 6:33 declares, "Seek ye first the Kingdon of God and his righteousness, and all these things will be added unto you."

CHAPTER 24

Frank Carter (1944–2021)
Profile of a Life[4]

Frank Carter was the only child born to Willie D. and Willie Lee "Boykin" Carter in Alabama on December 29, 1944. He came to Niagara Falls at a young age where he was raised in the church and was last a member of Trinity Baptist Church.

He graduated from Niagara Falls High School, where he played football, basketball, and ran track, where he held the high jump record for many years. Ignoring the advice of his high school counselor to "just join the army," Frank attended Roberts Wesleyan College on an academic scholarship and received his bachelor's degree in 1967. At Roberts, he ran track and led the 1964–1967 basketball teams to championships. They became the most successful sports team in the history of the school. Frank and his teammates were inducted into the Hall of Fame in 2019. He still holds the single-game scoring record of 54 (before 3-point baskets). He also held multiple track records, including triple jump and high jump.

After graduating from Roberts, Frank received his master's degree in teaching from Niagara University. He was a history and sometimes math teacher at North Junior High School, where he taught the first-ever black history class in Niagara Falls. Frank was

---

4 Taken from program at Frank Carter's funeral.

also a dedicated coach. He coached the boys' track team, and during the summers, he was a coach at the Niagara University Basketball Camp, the camp that was run by his friend, NBA Pro Calvin Murphy.

Frank continued to play basketball at the Eldridge Club, where he led his team, the Al Maroones, to many championships. He also enjoyed bowling in several tournaments and leagues where he led his teams to championships and recorded several perfect three-hundred games.

After teaching, he went to work at DuPont for many years and eventually retired after making many more lifelong friends. Ever the sports aficionado, he could be spotted at local sporting events. When he wasn't watching sports or news on television, he enjoyed traveling or going to the movie theater.

Frank was kind, compassionate, and known for his unique hair. He had a great sense of humor that drew people to him. He was a loving husband and father who instilled in his children the importance of education and encouraged them to play sports.

He is survived by his children Sheri, Michele, Frank M., Jamie, and grandchildren Adrienne, Nah'Qui, Frank M., Jr., Vince, Christopher, Camden, and Cameron. He was predeceased by his wife, Lynda, and grandson Joshua.

Bill Bachmann

Bill Bachmann was one of the most gifted people I ever met. He became a world-class commercial photographer, and he had some of the largest corporations in the world as clients. He traveled to all the world's continents to create beautiful images for his clients.

He came to Roberts from Pittsburgh in 1963. He would become the All-Time leading career rebounder at the school. He also held the record for single-season rebounds per game, plus many other records. Bill was very capable of playing Division I ball.

Bill loved this team, and he loved Coach Hughes. This team probably has had more reunions than any other athletic team at Roberts. Bill was the person who made the reunions happen. Sadly, we lost Bill to pancreatic cancer in 2017. Fortunately, he was able to attend the Athletic Hall of Fame Induction Ceremony for the '65–'67 Basketball Team two weeks before he passed.

CHAPTER 25

Ken Curtis 1947–1970

Ken Curtis was one of the best basketball players ever to come out of John Marshall High School in Rochester, New York. He arrived at Roberts as the top recruit in the fall of 1965. He immediately made varsity his first year, no small feat considering the wealth of talent the team possessed. He earned plenty of playing time that year as well with his outstanding outside shooting and his ability to mix it up with the big guys underneath. Ken went on to have a solid career and averaged 25 points per game in his junior year.

After Ken graduated in 1969, he married Anne Schmalfuss (also class of '69). He took a job with Eastman Kodak and was relocated to Minnesota. Tragically, Ken and Anne were both killed in a car crash just a few weeks after they arrived. We will never forget Ken and Anne for their contributions to the life of the campus and their positive effect on their fellow students.

Dale Easterly

One of the most versatile players on the team and certainly one of the best defensive players, Dale was a key contributor to the '65–'67 team. Dale is a member of the Roberts Athletic Hall of Fame on an individual basis and as a member of the Hall of Fame Basketball Team. Sadly, we lost Dale to cancer in 2018.

CHAPTER 26

Harry Elmore Hutt (1942–2022)

Heaven changed forever on February 19, 2022, at 3:35 a.m., when Harry Hutt arrived and asked God, "Can I watch SportsCenter here?"

Harry was born July 15, 1942, in Gloversville, New York, to Rev. Herschel and Valentine Hutt. Sports always played a significant role in Harry's life. He played basketball, baseball, and soccer and was an all-star shot-putter in high school. For the next thirty years, he continued his love for sports, holding coaching and front-office executive positions in both college and professional athletics that included Spring Arbor University, Roberts Wesleyan College, University of Buffalo, Detroit Pistons, Portland Trailblazers, Seattle Seahawks, and Tamps Bay Lightning. He did it all—coaching marketing, ticket operations, broadcasting and media communications, corporate sales, and digital media. He lived life big and squeezed every last drop out of every moment.

Perhaps even more impressive was his teaching experience. He always said, "Teaching and mentoring are the main hallmarks of my sports career." He helped shape many young men's and women's lives, not only on how to have a successful career in sports but also how to be successful in life. And he continued to mentor them wherever they lived or wherever they worked.

Everywhere you looked in Harry's various homes across the US, there would be signed posters, basketballs, hockey sticks, and *really big* shoes from the likes of Bill Walton, Dennis Rodman, Bill Laimbeer, and Isiah Thomas. Harry never took off his Detroit Pistons championship ring. In fact, he had two (1989 and 1990) and would rotate wearing them. Even people in grocery stores would ask him about his ring, and he was more than happy to tell them about the "Bad Boys" and their back-to-back championships. He never met a stranger.

Generosity was Harry's middle name. You wanted tickets to a game or concert? Harry could set you up. He knew everyone! The friendships Harry made through the years continued right up until the end. His passion and enthusiasm for life were contagious, and he loved regaling friends and family with his stories, long and around the barn as they often were.

He loved his three daughters, Shawna, Allyson, and Vicki, as well as his eleven grandchildren and five great-grandchildren. His legacy to them is that "home" was always open to anyone needing a place to belong. His house was your house. He was proud of their achievements, was their biggest advocate, and loved visiting all of them in Michigan.

I, Dave, am thankful to be able to call Harry Hutt a lifelong friend. I met Harry when I was a freshman at Roberts. Never did I meet anyone who had such authority on sports and the credentials of the athletes who played the games. Harry was a giant in terms of sports knowledge. He was even bigger than that as a friend. I used to go over to his house and hang out, talking sports with Harry until after midnight. He always made me feel welcome.

I played basketball all four years at Roberts. During that time, Harry was an assistant coach and sports information director. He was a keen observer of everything that happened on and off the court. His opinions were highly valued. He had a remarkable ability to validate all athletic activity, and he had a tremendous gift for marketing and promoting sports. During his time as sports information director, Roberts Wesleyan teams received prodigious press coverage in the two Rochester newspapers.

After Harry and his first wife moved to Spring Arbor, Michigan, he became ready to hone his skills on a bigger stage. I told Harry of an opening for an assistant coach at the University of Buffalo, and he got the job.

The work he did at the University of Buffalo provided Harry with the springboard he needed to get into professional sports. He joined the Buffalo Braves of the NBA and quickly demonstrated his superior ability to sell and market. From the Buffalo Braves, he went to the Detroit Pistons, and the rest is history.

Harry and I crossed paths several times over the years. He never had his roots. When my basketball team was named the best team in the history of Roberts Wesleyan College and inducted (as a team) into the Roberts Athletic Hall of Fame, Harry was asked to make the player introductions to an assembled crowd. His vast institutional memory and his poignant wit proved that he was the best person to do this job as he entertained and educated the crowd. I was so motivated by this experience that I wrote an article about my personal fifty-year journey to the Roberts Athletic Hall of Fame. It was published in the Roberts Wesleyan Alumni Newsletter. Harry edited the article, and he made significant suggestions that made the article much better.

Harry was a friend and mentor to me. I miss his humor, his friendship, and his commentary. May God be with his family, and may Harry rest in peace. He was one of a kind.

Harry Hutt's Celebration of Life Story from memorial pamphlet.

Summary

In the opening lines of this book, I indicated that outstanding performance (whether it occurs in sports, business, or academics) does not just happen. There are reasons and factors that drive outstanding performance. One of the goals of this book was to identify the reasons and factors that drove the 1965–67 men's basketball team at Roberts Wesleyan College to perform as it did.

All coaches are interested in top performance and how to make it happen. I submit that there are often myriad reasons why great performance is achieved. However, I believe that great performance is a function of a well-thought-out system. In sports, this system is usually developed over time by an astute coach who is a student of the game and totally dedicated to winning. A good system has many moving parts, and there is a reason for each part to exist. Each part complements the other parts. When all these parts function together, the performance of the team is like a well-engineered and well-tuned car going smoothly down the road while getting great gas mileage.

When there is no system, or the system in place is not well-designed with parts that are not functioning well, the results are a bumpy ride with poor gas mileage. We have all seen many athletic teams that look like this car.

Here is my opinion as to why we were a great performing team. We had a system. It was carefully designed by Coach Hughes. Here are some of the components of Coach Hughes' system:

- *Barriers to performance were identified and removed.* Whatever got in the way of the team's ability to perform was quickly identified and removed.
- *Clear expectations were communicated.* Everyone knew exactly where to be on the court for all offensive and defensive sets, as well as what his job was.
- *There were consequences.* These consequences existed for good performance and poor performance. Good performance led to more playing time; poor performance led to more time on the bench.
- *There was a lot of feedback.* Coach Hughes showered us with lots of statistics, including our own individual and team statistics. If we were getting behind in any statistical category, he let us know in no uncertain terms.
- *There was a vision. In the Bible, it says, "Without vision, the people perish." Good coaches have a vision and communicate it well. Coach Hughes painted a picture in our brains of being at the national tournament in Kansas City.*
- *There was detailed preparation. Coach Hughes embodied preparation, whether it was scouting the opposition, planning practice, or creating a game plan.*

Conclusions

Here is my attempt to answer the question of why was this team so good:

- Coach Hughes was unquestionably the right man for the job.
- It helped to have an All-American, Frank Carter.
- The team had the all-time scorer and leading rebounder on the roster.
- Coach Hughes delivered the all-time recruiting coup when he convinced Frank Carter to come to Roberts.
- The team was composed of outstanding people of character.
- There was no selfishness, no playground soloists.
- Frank Carter was a great leader on and off the court. He made his teammates better.
- A vision was presented by the coach, and the team bought into it.
- We had tremendous fans who supported and motivated us.
- We had great support from the college.

In the final analysis, I believe that Coach Hughes was the most important factor in the team's success. One could argue that Frank Carter should be named as the most important factor. There is no question that Frank took us a long way and that he was the greatest player in the school's history. But if there was no Coach Hughes, there would have been no Frank Carter. You may beg to differ, and that's fine. But that's the way I see it.

The 1966–1967 Athletic Hall of Fame team induction.
Left to right: Harry Hutt, Keith Moore, Stan Ziblut, Ralph
Roach, Dale Easterly, Herm Schwingle, Darwin Chapman,
Frank Carter, Glenn Schultz, Noel Smith, Paul Crowell, Paul
Mroz, Dave Scribner, Bill Bachmann, Coach Bill Hughes.

In Memoria

Frank Carter
Bill Bachmann
Ken Curtis
Dale Easterly
Harry Hutt
Noel Smith

Voices of Roberts

The Greatest Era: A Team to Know: Men's Basketball 1965-67

There is no greater honor for any athletic team than to be recognized as the greatest of its era. The 1965-67 Roberts Wesleyan College men's basketball team took time to grow and nurture into this lasting legacy, realizing it goes beyond individual players and team stats. These young men, most Hall of Famers in their own right, learned to fill their role for the success of the entire team. Led by Coach Bill Hughes, they learned to communicate well, focus on goals and results, support each other, and develop a mentoring culture and become good leaders. They became a brotherhood where everyone contributed to their fair share, felt a sense of belonging, and were committed to the team's success. What an example, especially for today's student-athletes.

It was a special era for Roberts Wesleyan men's basketball. Basketball fever was at its peak and over-capacity crowds were often the case. Because Roberts has no suitable gymnasium, games were played in the Churchville Chili high school gym. For the game against regional powerhouse Buffalo State, parking lots overflowed with fans hours before game time. When the team returned from the NAIA playoffs, students and community members lined the streets around campus to welcome the players. "It was the best time to be a Raider." Team member Stan Ziblet '66 said.

The seeds were planted and nurtured in 1964-65 under the leadership of Coach Hughes when the team was 14-6. Their record was 18-4 in 1965-66 and they came back the next season — during the college's 100th year — with a 20-5 record that included an incredible run of 16 straight victories, numerous school records and the first Monroe County Tournament Championship, which would go on to run for 50 years and become the longest in-season tournament in the country.

This era of the men's basketball program has a lasting significance on the Robert's Wesleyan campus, where the memories echo in the arena and create inspiration for future student-athletes. Current athletes walk in the footsteps and reflect on the preparation and hard work of these players. It is not only about being remembered for these legacies, but also setting a lasting example of respect, love and true meaning of teamwork that will never fade away.

Led by Coach Hughes, the members of the 1965-1967 Roberts Wesleyan College men's basketball era represent value, community, and God's faithfulness. The team included:

> Coach Bill Hughes
> Bob Ahlin '66
> Bill Bachmann '67
> Frank Carter '67
> Darwin Chapman '69
> Paul Crowell '69
> Ken Curtis '69
> Dale Easterly '68
> Harry Hutt '65
> Keith Moore '67
> Paul Mroz '69 (Manager)
> Ralph Roach '71
> Glen Schultz '68
> Herm Schwingle '67
> Dave Scribner '69
> Noel Smith '68
> Stan Zibult '66

A Rhyme to Noel Smith

Don't like pain; don't like strife.
Don' l like it when a friend goes under the knife.

But that's what he did, coming out like new.
He's loved by his teammates; they call him Big Blue

We'll never forget his skills on the court.
How he banged the boards, never came up short
As good as he was, he's an even better guy.
You're in our prayers, and that' no lie.

Your Friend,

Dave
March 9, 2024

Just before this book went to press, we received the sad news of Noel Smith's passing. I was fortunate to be the last non-family member to speak with him. Noel and I grew up in Batavia, NY, and, as mentioned in Chapter 5, we were teammates on a Babe Ruth League team. Noel was fiercely loyal to his friends, and I was lucky to count him among my best friends. He was incredibly helpful as I wrote this book. I gave him a copy of my original manuscript, sensing he might not make it to the publication date. He and his wife, Winnie, read it together in the hospital. I was thrilled when he told me it was a great read.

We will all miss Noel deeply; he was a very special person.

AFTERWORD

It has been a privilege for me to write this book. During the data-collection phase of the project, I thoroughly enjoyed reconnecting with my teammates as well as many other individuals who had intimate knowledge of the team and its players. Special thanks go to Keith Moore for leading me to 1969 World Series star Ron Swoboda. I would like to give a huge shout-out to one of my best friends, Paul Mroz. He was so helpful in all phases of this project, especially technical support.

I enjoyed talking to Coach Hughes for hours on the phone. Sometimes, we would go for a couple of hours. That man can remember more details from fifty years ago than a fifty-gigabyte memory card.

My purpose in writing the book was to document how truly outstanding the team was. I hope I have accomplished that goal. Many thanks go to my wife, Mary Kay, for being such a great supporter during this project. I could not have done it without her. Finally, I would like to thank Roberts Wesleyan University for providing me with the opportunity to represent the school as a member of the '65–'67 Raiders.

Thank you for reading this book.

Dave Scribner
February 2024

Photographs courtesy of Rebecca McColl, Executive Director of Institutional Advancement Roberts Wesleyan University and Paul Mroz
Also noteworthy of mention is Bob Ahlin on the 1965-1966 team who averaged 1.6 points per game and 2.3 rebounds per game.

APPENDIX A

1965-66 VARSITY STATISTICS

NAME	GAMES PLAYED	FG	FGA	FG PFT.	FT	FTA	FT PCT.	REB	AVG.	T.P.	AVG.
Frank Carter	22	229	495	.462	98	121	.809	227	10.3	556	25.2
Stan Zibult	22	72	169	.425	24	41	.604	74	3.4	168	7.6
Bill Bachmann	22	166	348	.477	66	94	.702	330	15.0	398	18.0
Keith Moore	22	103	225	.457	44	69	.637	92	4.1	250	11.3
Herm Schwingle	17	46	144	.320	24	39	.615	59	3.4	118	7.0
Glenn Schultz	22	36	97	.371	24	38	.631	72	3.2	96	4.3
Dale Easterly	22	38	74	.513	31	41	.756	50	2.2	107	4.8
Noel Smith	20	27	60	.450	12	20	.600	101	5.0	66	3.3
Bob Ahlin	13	9	33	.275	3	9	.333	31	2.3	21	1.6
Ken Curtis	16	35	94	.372	17	28	.607	64	4.0	87	6.4
Dave Scribner	2	0	3	.000	0	1	.000	0	0	0	0
TEAM REBOUNDS								130	5.9		
RWC TOTALS	22	762	1742	.437	343	501	.684	1230	55.9	1867	84.8
OPPONENTS TOTALS	22	620	1527	.406	341	538	.633	1012	46.0	1581	71.8

APPENDIX B

1966-67 VARSITY BASKETBALL STATISTICS

NAME	GP	FGM	FGA	FG%	FTM	FTA	FT%	REB.	R. AVE.	PTS.	P. AVE.
Carter	25	251	551	.455	120	167	.718	252	10.1	622	24.8
Bachmann	25	206	389	.529	70	132	.530	336	13.4	482	19.2
Moore	25	116	293	.395	50	81	.617	92	3.6	282	11.2
Schultz	25	97	247	.392	37	69	.536	161	6.4	231	9.2
Curtis	25	86	232	.371	58	81	.716	148	5.9	230	9.2
Easterly	25	53	120	.442	52	88	.591	106	4.2	158	6.3
Smith	25	39	107	.364	25	40	.625	155	6.2	103	4.1
Scribner	25	32	82	.390	34	53	.642	34	1.3	98	3.9
Crowell	15	16	25	.640	10	15	.666	32	2.1	42	2.8
Roach	11	5	17	.294	5	15	.333	8	0.7	15	1.3
Chapman	12	0	7	.000	2	3	.666	8	0.6	2	0.1
TEAM REBOUNDS								186	7.4		
TOTALS		901	2079	.433	463	748	.618	1518	60.7	2266	90.6

ABOUT THE AUTHOR

Dave Scribner (M.A. Michigan State) was well-positioned to author this book as he not only played basketball at Roberts Wesleyan but also coached there after graduating in 1969. He considers the opportunity to play on the '65–'67 teams to be one of the greatest experiences of his life.

Dave and his wife Mary Kay, whom he met at Roberts, have been married 48 years. They reside in Fairport, New York. They have three grown children and six grandchildren. Dave considers the opportunity to spend time with his grandchildren to be as special as playing basketball. Dave also enjoys photography and golf as his hobbies.

The idea for writing a book came to Dave when the team was chosen as the greatest team in the history of the college in 2017. Every living player and coach made it back to Roberts for the induction ceremony. At that time, Dave realized what a special team this was and that the team's achievements should be documented and celebrated for posterity.

Printed in the USA
CPSIA information can be obtained
at www.ICGtesting.com
CBHW021758060924
14141CB00005B/88

9 798893 456585